Opening Prayer and Scripture

God forgive us for all of our inequities even though life throws inequalities. For we realize that pressure produces diamonds, give us strength to endure. As we are overcomers, more than conquers clear our vision so that we are able to see ourselves as you go. We are the authority and have been more than equipped to dominate the principalities of this world. Lord, we cannot do this alone but by your spirit o' God we shall move. Thank you for reminding us that, we shall not die, but live and declare the works of the Lord.

Psalms 118:17

CONTENTS

Prelude 1

Mirrors 3

Chapter 1 5

Chapter 2 10

Chapter 3 21

Chapter 4 30

Chapter 5 35

Chapter 6 41

Chapter 7 46

Chapter 8 53

Chapter 9 62

Chapter 10 73

Chapter 11 87

Chapter 12 94

Chapter 13 103

Chapter 14 107

Chapter 15 114

Chapter 16 122

Chapter 17 129

Chapter 18 138

Chapter 19 151

Chapter 20 163

Chapter 21 196

Chapter 22 214

PRELUDE

I sat down and took a deep breath; today is the day that I write my story. For so long I'd searched for help outside of myself. Due to distorted views of myself and misguided self-efficacy my life took several major twists and turns, each spiraling into dysfunctional behaviors of me trying to save myself by hiding myself. Should my memory serve me as correct, it was Walter Scott who stated, *"O' what a tangled web we weave when we first practice to deceive!"* Ouch! That burns; the truth sure does hurt even when we're unable to realize what truth really is. Life sure does go on. Life doesn't take a break to allow you to catch up or realize reality or wait for you to reach an understanding… Life keeps moving. So, understanding that Life keeps moving we must also grasp the concept of, as long as we allow ourselves to operate in a mindset of trauma we are deceiving ourselves and that deception grows as our lives and the lives around us are moving forward. Ok, let's expound on that a little. Operating in a traumatic state of mind, whether we know it or not most of us are on autopilot; our thoughts and actions are developed paradigms that were generated at the time of our conception formulated by our parents or household dynamics and honed as we became responsible for ourselves. With that understanding in mind, we create our lives according to that structure; that example of living life. This design can either be a blessing or a curse or dare I say both; a blessing and a curse.

 This is a story of Victory! My story speaks about the traumas that were created before our conception and thus born into. I walk through different phases of my experiences addressing the inability to cope with physical and psychological pain in healthy ways. This story isn't for the squeamish or faint of heart. This is one bold revelation that must be told as we all shall live and not die! In the words of Katt Williams, "Winners are not allowed to let losers rewrite history (my story)."

I've always been a person who loves to write; especially after being introduced to poetry forms such as Haikus in the seventh-grade. I remember my first poem vividly, *The Way the Wind Blows*." While I will not recite it; I do remember the experience that I felt as I wrote it. I imagined a tree; an Oak tree to be exact swaying in the wind. Who knew that my life would be just that; a sway in the wind? I found myself in odd places doing strange things with a deep desire to live. To live?

MIRRORS

Growing up I didn't have a lot of positive role models. My life has been a great experiment of growth. I have had several inspirational teachers that poured bitter-sweet waters into my soul; because of them I am awake.

In my house there were no mirrors just images of faded, distorted dreams. In my house there was no laughter, just faint cries of bitterness and heartbreak. Screams and roars from drug addicted beasts. As the doors slam my body cringes for peace. My mind creates a place warm, and bright to escape to.

As I grew restless for a better existence, I began my experiment of joy and success by any means necessary. I traveled many miles as I was born to do. I explored the living and the things that the living do. Walking down a dark, clouded path I got lost in the streets. A young woman, not as big as a flea, with heart as big as the sea… somebody had to rescue me.

There were no mirrors in my house just pictures of faded, distorted dreams. Broken glass releases the cold, chilling truth; you cannot recapture your youth and your present day sends you into dismay. Sighs, of what to do. Breaths of who to blame. Frowns of shame. And you lived thinking that life was a game.

When my heart was broken from harsh words spoken through time… I damn near lost my mind. Torn and broken, knee bent and hell bound, destined to where those shame frowns, I was low; low as the ground. When an Angel called my name, "Princess," too lost to look up until I heard my name again, "Princess." I looked up and there he was. He stood 5'11.5", with warm brown eyes, chocolate skin, with a friendly grin. He reached for me with one hand and held a Bible in the other. He ministered to my broken spirit and kissed life into my heart. He walked a path that I followed which led me to today and opening up my tomorrow. I am awake.

I have mirrors in my house with prosperous dreams and laughter, no screams. I have colors in my house red, yellow, purple and green. There are flowers in my home, now there is no reason for me to roam. I have Love in my Heart and I know... Love and I will never part. There is warmth and tranquility in my house as God lives there. I can sleep and a perfect sleep as I am safe with a peace that passes all understanding. I. Have. Mirrors. In. My. House. And they reflect Laughter and Smiles.

Chapter 1

I wrote the poem *Mirrors* when I was in my early twenties. I would sit down in my room, turn on a nice tune by Erykah Badu; preferably *Orange Moon*. As Erykah bellowed the words, "I'm brighter than before…" I would imagine myself smiling and shining as the sun rays bounced off of my ebony skin and feeling the vibrations. I would imagine myself happy. By this time, I was already a single mother of two; without an education. Yep, no high school diploma; working dead-end job after job on welfare and Section 8…No hope for my future so I thought; unless GOD adhered to my prayers and sent me a man to take me away from my dismay. There I was, searching outside of myself for all of the answers.

I found myself on a road I'd developed as a child; looking for love in all the wrong places. Looking back I never really had an understanding of how valuable I was. Being molested and silenced took away my power; took away my understanding of truth. My family had considered me to be liar; I later understood that calling me liar kept them from having to face their truths. My mom would pretty much lock me in our house; I could only go out for school, grocery and church. Occasionally, I was allowed to sit on my front porch. I'd made my bedroom my shell; my safe place.

Being molested is like murder and if you have never been molested or raped you'll never truly understand. It took me half my life to regain myself and to actually start to live my life after experiencing the traumas of molestation and rape. The most damaging thing was not having any one in my corner and nowhere to run. My grandmother told me one night when I was about 12 years old; "…if you ever want them to stop crawling in your room at night sleep with a butcher's knife…and when they come show them that you got it." That let me know right there, that everyone knew what was happening to me and it was up to me to stop it. I did exactly that; I stopped it…but something inside of me changed.

Self-destruction was the spirit that I'd inhabited without knowing. I had hopes, dreams and aspirations but they were diminished by the tortures of all that I'd allowed myself to go through because I didn't know any other way. My mental health was always mocked in my household. Throughout my childhood I was called names like *crazy, wild, fast* etc. I heard these things so often until I started to believe that I was crazy and wild. I was too afraid to be "fast" but I was promiscuous in a sense as I didn't know how to say "NO." Hmmm, what if I were told how beautifully intelligent I am, how graceful and loved I am… what a difference life may have been for us all.

My Aunt Pamela would always call me the prettiest black girl she'd seen. As I grew, she'd tell me that I should explore a career as a model. I didn't know why she would such things to me as I had not a clue how delightfully sublime I was. I knew that I was kind of cute but pretty enough to model; yeah right. At any rate, just hearing my aunt say those words to me was a major confident changer; if only for a moment. The highlight of my days were getting out of school and clocking into work- getting off from work and going to the club with my older girlfriends. I love music and I absolutely need to dance.

My momma called me Chrissy a few times; yes Chrissy from the television show *Three's Company*. I was tall for my age, socially awkward and quite clumsy. Ya know? I am still quite clumsy; I bump into everything. Hey, I get a good laugh out of it though and so do the on lookers. I've been called names like Olive Oyl-skinny with big breast, Torpedo-my mom bought me old lady bras and they made my breasts stick out like missiles. I didn't like those names but hey I didn't take ownership of the name that I'd been given so it's a free for all.

"*What's In a Name*?" William Shakespeare asks in the timeless romance of Romeo and Juliet. I didn't feel like a Princess…I didn't feel like much of anything or anyone. But hey, what a thought provoking question? Four words that will guide one's thought process into self-discovery. It took me a while to get it; yet I got it.

Before, I just jump right into the real life of being young, gifted, economically challenged and black; let me tell you a story of a girl who cried tears that she never understood. A story of a girl who feared no-one but herself and her momma. A young lady developing into a menace to society with eyes wide shut. Yes, that is me.

As a teenager, I thought I had my life all figure out. I was maybe fourteen or fifteen and just knew I had what it took to make it in this world. I was mature enough to attend school without my mother having to wake me. I was mature enough to care for a house full of kids; almost better than any adult that I knew. I worked a full-time job and I bought my own clothes. Yep, I was ready for the world. Huh, the joke was on whom; me, that's who.

Reformation of a Queen

Man, I can remember waking up in bed with two thousand and one thoughts racing in my head. So much to do in so little time, I just knew I was losing my mind.

Each day I approached as if I had died the day before. I knew what I wanted and knew how to get it…but where would I obtain it?

My mission; I had made too complexed, you see. Dang! What was sometimes obvious to you was a mystery to me. And the funny thing is; this is me. I made a statement once, "I never travel through one thought." It's true.

My mind is so open and free, there are no boundaries within me. I think about many things on many different levels. I focus. Because I focus on three different subjects and other objects, do you think I am losing my mind?

Life tried to ball me up, chew me up, and spit me out…but I just wouldn't crumble. My father abandoned a flower to be raped and abused, at other times missed used. My Mother with God's help reformed a Queen.

I was born with the thunder and lightning; Sounds descending loud and proud as Cassandra Wilson would snap…The sun kissed my tears…The moon healed my hurts…The stars held my opportunities…I reached for them and now I am redeemed.

Through many of life's adversities I have stood, I am standing, I will stand.

Strong is my spirit, complexed is my mental…misunderstood by those who approach me with a carnal mind. Yet, I have risen above troubled waters just to face the plight of another day. Still I look forward to it. Hope is what my heart is made of.

Today I am born. My eyes are open to where they once were shut. I can see the road clear. I know exactly where I am headed. People and their issues seem so different now…Since my head is above the water; Conscious!

I am awake…I can no longer sleep. I have been saved from "The Destruction of the African-American Civilization." I have built my house on the highest hill in the village near the horizon. I have begun the birth of a tribe. A tribe of myself…Love!

Chapter 2

S.H.E. was Born May 23, 1980, in Jacksonville, Florida in University Hospital to Cynthia Brown and Billy Booker; a bald-headed chocolate baby girl. My parents weren't married at the time so I inherited my mother's surname Brown; which she obtained from a previous marriage. At the time of my birth, my father was deployed as a fairly new Navy Sergeant. The story told is that my father was on the phone during my birth and named me Princess after a girl that he'd grown up with. I do not recall my adolescent years prior to four years old; so growing up in a two-parent household is not memory. My father abandoned our family when I was four years old. He'd left my mom, my brother and me in a small town in Texas. My grandmother says that her parents had to drive from Florida to Texas to rescue us from despair. Like I said, I really do not recall much prior to moving to Florida; yet the Chronicles of S.H.E. was formed.

My first memories starts with growing up in Silver Creek Apartments which wasn't so bad. I was able to roam the neighborhood freely; it was the '80s. My friends and I would play dodge ball, hop scotch and make mud pies. My favorite activity was break-dancing with my cousin Michael and doing random childish things around the projects with my cousin Snookie. Wait, like the time it was pouring down raining outside and Snookie had gotten soaked. He knew that he couldn't enter his momma's house wet, so he asked me to walk over to the community laundromat with him. I did as asked; I mean he was my big cousin and he always had all of the best snacks and came up with the best outdoor games. We walked to the laundromat and we found ourselves standing in front of the dryers. I had no idea why we were standing there. Snookie looked over at me and said,

"Cuz, I have two quarters. When I get in the dryer, put one quarter in that lil' slot and then push the start button right there. When I knock on the glass hurry up and open the door so I can get out."

I nodded.

Snookie climbed inside the dryer, and I did what he told me. After a while, he knocked on the door from the inside of the dryer. It took me extra effort and time to open the door because I was so small at the time. I finally managed to open it though.

Wow, he's a genius. I thought to myself as Snookie jumped out almost all dry.

"Why didn't you hurry up?" Snookie asked immediately.

Snookie turned and again asked me, "Why didn't you hurry up and open the door?"

I replied, "I was trying but the door was stuck." Snookie rolled his eyes which showed his revulsion toward my response.

"Am I dry enough?" He asked.

"Not all the way," I said, scanning him from top to bottom.

"At least it's not as bad as it was. Let's go back before Momma gets off from work." We left the laundromat as if what we'd done was completely normal.

This is just an example of how we used to have fun there. And for someone like me, who had gone through emotional trauma at such an early age, such moments felt liberating.

How about the time when I visited my friend who lived adjacent to a grumpy old white man and I parked my brand new Strawberry Shortcake bike on their shared porch? As I knocked on my friend's door hoping that she was able to come out and play.

"Get your damn bike off of my porch," said the grumpy old white man as he'd opened his door and threw my bicycle in the dirt.

I was very angry and I responded, "Imma go get my cousin Snookie and we gonna beat your ass."

Now the language I used would not have been approved by my mom but my cousins taught me to be tough. It was hell growing up in the projects without a backbone.

I picked up my bike and rode around until I found my cousin. Now Snookie was only a few years older than I. We went back around there and stormed that man's door with our fist screaming out all sorts of obscene words. Looking back, the man was only frustrated because we were so rude and the once quiet neighborhood had turned into *"The Hood"* if you know what I mean.

It was the early 1980s; crack cocaine had hit the streets all across America. The city of Jacksonville was no exception. The influx of cocaine powder caused approximately an 80% drop in street value. Drug dealers being faced with the issue of losing profit, came up with the idea to convert the cocaine powder into *crack*, a solid form of cocaine that could be smoked versus snorted. Crack was a street hustler's dream as it produces an instant high and its users become addicted in a very short time. I've heard some crack addicts say that the first smoke got them hooked as they are always chasing that initial "high"/feeling.

The biggest surge in the use of the drug occurred during the "crack epidemic" between 1984 and 1990, when the drug spread across American cities. The crack epidemic dramatically increased the number of Americans addicted to cocaine. In 1985, the number of people who admitted to using cocaine on a routine basis increased from 4.2 million to 5.8 million. Unfortunately, my mother as well as so many others in my family were amongst that 5.8 million. When my mom first started smoking crack cocaine, my brother and I were completely oblivious. Life was life and all we knew was mom was having a bit of a hard time being a single mom and all. However, in the projects 95% of the households consisted of single mothers having a hard time; we were all struggling and didn't know it. Hell, the 5% of the homes with fathers/boyfriends/live-ins were struggling too.

Reminiscing on the lyrics of a popular song at that time; "Your momma's on crack rock." "No, not my momma." As my mother's addiction grew beyond her control our home started to crumble. It's funny the things that you remember, like the time Ms. Sherry came to our house to confront my mom about a drug deal gone wrong or what have you. I was sitting on the stairs attempting to play Jackstones; I was horrible at the game.

As I'd started to get frustrated I saw Ms. Sherry walking towards our apartment. She made her way up the stairs, walked pass me without even speaking. In a sarcastic voice, I mumbled, "Hey Ms. Sherry." She knocked at our door with frustration. My mom opened the door and kindly asked her to leave. While the conversation they were having is a blur, I can recall the angry hand gestures. Ms. Sherry was pointing her finger at mom and yelling loudly. My momma said, "Sherry as long as you don't touch me we alright; so gon' and leave." Ms. Sherry's index finger touched my momma's shoulder and from there it was all she wrote. My mom picked Ms. Sherry up and body slammed her. See what Ms. Sherry did not know, my momma used to be a welterweight female boxer in Bethstuy, New York. My mom beat Ms. Sherry something terrible. I even got a few licks in, which I regretted later because my mom got on my behind for doing so.

After the fight was over, Ms. Sherry gathered her bearings and made her way back to her mother's house in Caravan Apartments that were adjacent from our apartment complex, Silver Creek. It was on from there. You see Ms. Sherry was the sister of a well-known crime family. Less than 20 minutes had gone by from the time Ms. Sherry had left our house, two car loads of men drove up and jumped out from their cars. They ran up our stairs and banged at our door. My mother was adamant about keeping the door locked. My cousin Michael, who was 15 years old at the time, had come over for a visit. My granddaddy Allen had stopped by as well. As the men were knocking at our door, my mother was explaining to my granddaddy that the men had come for her because she'd just been in a fight with Ms. Sherry. My granddaddy wanted to reason with the angry mob of men. My mother pleaded with him to not open the door; he opened the door anyway.

The violent men came rushing through the door. My mother fought them as best she as she could. There were at least five men attacking my mom at one time. My momma had a mean left hook and she was using every ounce of it. My cousin Michael was fighting about three men himself until an older gentleman pulled out what seemed to be the biggest knife I'd ever seen and put it to my cousin's throat while ordering my momma to stop fighting or he would kill my cousin. I saw the look of defeat in my momma's eyes. She stopped fighting and the angry mob beat my mother something fierce. That day, I swore that no one would ever hurt my mom again… No one!

Dear momma, why'd it have to be so rough? As time went by, the crack epidemic had taken its toll on much of the neighborhood. From drug dealers, to addicts, to violence…it all became life for us. Escaping was never a thought for me; I just wanted to know how to use the "Game" to my advantage and make my family better. It never occurred to me that there was another way to live for a brown skinned girl like ME.

You see, what life was for some other girl at that time was different from mine. I never thought about what it would be like to live on the other side. I just wanted to come up so that the other kids in the neighborhood would stop picking on me and my brother. I wanted all the adults to stop putting their mouths on my mother. Yeah, our female neighbors had a lot to say about my mom at the time. Yeah Cynt; my momma, was on crack and it had become quite apparent that she was losing a grip. Needless to say, those same women were coming to see my mom for help; as they'd gone through all of their food stamps and/or welfare benefits for the month and their sugar daddies were nowhere to be found which left them wanting… yeah, they needed food. However, I digress as I get a little bitter about this part.

I can't remember my exact age but I remember my mom having company over. It was a classmate that she'd known more than half her life; Melvin or "Mr. Melvin" is what we called him. That night, my mom and Mr. Melvin shared a few laughs, smoked a little weed; they chatted about old times. The night came upon them and mom had asked Mr. Melvin to leave. He bellowed a chuckle that was a weird awkward sound and I could hear the shakiness in my mom's voice as she repeated herself, asking Mr. Melvin to leave. I heard Mr. Melvin begin to sing, "Eb, Ebenezer…" I can still hear this song in my nightmares. By this time, my mother was crying and begging him to stop. "Come on now Melvin. Don't do this. My kids are in the other room; please Melvin, no don't do this to me." I just remember her crying all night long.

My brother and I were in my bedroom which was close to our living room. I could see and hear everything. We were devastated. As our mother lay on our sofa crying tears of despair; my brother and I were in my room balling our eyes out. We were too young to fully understand what had happened yet we understood exactly what had happened. Trauma…never discussed; never acknowledged. Yet, it festers inside of each us, torturing us.

As time progressed, my mother decided to check herself into a drug rehabilitation facility. My goodness, a child without a mother in the hands of a dysfunctional family is bad; let alone two children. Once my momma decided to check herself into the rehabilitation facility, she entrusted us with our Aunt Birdie. At the time, Aunt Birdie was a pretty cool person, so we thought. She had one child, my cousin Ariel. I can't quite remember how old Ariel was when all of this took place but she's 3 years younger than me. My Aunt Birdie needed a place to stay so she and my mom agreed that my aunt would move into our place and care for us during her stint in rehab. What my mother didn't know was that my Aunt Birdie was battling an addiction of her own. Yep, she was addicted to crack cocaine too. So, the saga continues.

During my mom's stint in Rehab things were beginning to be revealed. Stories were starting to be shared through verbal as well as non-verbal communication all while my brother and I were in the midst. It was like they didn't care how we felt as they discussed my mother in such a negative light. I once heard my Aunt Birdie ridicule my mom for smoking crack; she once made a statement that went something like this, "Cynt, gon' tell me that 'Gain took her in the woods and at gunpoint raped and her forced her to hit the pipe." Now my mom had confided in her sister and look what she did. Now imagine hearing that your mom had been raped at gunpoint by your uncle and forced to smoke crack before you could even understand what all of that meant. Conversations such as this were only one of many.

My mom was away for quite a while; my brother and I were left in the care of our maternal relatives, those related through our mother's side of the family. While we knew and loved everyone; it never felt quite right being there. We were provided with food made with soulful Southern flare. We would play games with our cousins and friends. And boy, we would sing and dance…those were the good times. Then there were those dark days; when physical abuse took command of the atmosphere and tears would flow and dreams would become shattered. Further dismay, that there was no way out, I'd stop believing so. My family's expression of love was often tied to food. For example, my grandfather would say things like, "You gotta know that we love ya'll; we clothed and feed ya!" Statements such as that were spoken so often, I'd started to believe that and associate love with food and what someone does for me…tangible. Miseducation can be damning.

As I mentioned earlier, I have a younger brother, Nathan. He's two years younger than me and we shared what some would call a 'healthy relationship.' Nathan was an extrovert. We went to the same school at one point and while I struggled to make friends, Nathan adjusted himself pretty nicely. He not only made new friends but also had a confident personality. I was never jealous of him but sometimes criticized myself for not being like him. He was clearly the more charismatic child.

There came a time when Nathan got into drugs. He didn't just become a user but also began dealing. But that did not change my perspective about how he was as a person. I guess it was the circumstances that led him to that path. I will say this, however, that it wasn't only me who suffered. Yes, maybe my life was extremely difficult, but so was Nathan's. We witnessed our mother's mental and physical health deteriorate. My brother's presence somewhat lessened the pain.

Of all my family relationships, the one I had with my grandmother was the best. She was the one person I could always rely on. When my entire family called me a liar, she was beside me. She may not have actively done anything to prevent it, but I get that. My grandmother is what I'd call a silent warrior. Ol' Mrs. Martha didn't play no games but she had a heart that was etched in giving.

My relationship with my granny is so prevalent because without her and my grandfather, I would probably be a villain with a secret lair; just kidding but seriously. My grandma Martha was the first Black Woman to purchase a home in Royal Palm Beach (Atlantic Beach, FL) while raising four girls with an abusive and cheating husband. Can you imagine the shock when I found out that my granny picked cotton in Swainsboro, Georgia at the age of 4? Four years old with a sack 'cross her tiny neck charged with the task of picking enough cotton to fill it up; my goodness! My granny was born in 1939 in Swainsboro, GA. Her mother Daisy had 14 children if I'm not mistaken; three of them from her first husband and the others by her second husband Osie. My great-grandmother Daisy and her husband Osie moved their family to Jacksonville Beach, Florida to escape the violence brewing in the town from the Klu Klux Klan...yep the KKK. I didn't find this out until I was 40 years old.

My grandma Martha had four children and two marriages by the time she 19 years old. She finished high school, worked two jobs and raised her children with the help of her parents along with her sisters and brothers. I once asked her if there was anything about her life that she would like to have changed, and she said to me that she'd only wish that her faith in God was stronger earlier on in her life. I watched my grandmother keep a family together when no one else was concerned or cared. My grandfather was addicted to crack cocaine, three of her brothers were, two of her daughters were addicts, her grandchildren were selling crack and being delinquents. But, she would get up every morning get dressed for work, prepare a pot of coffee, drink one cup and head out the door. She'd come home from work, prepare a meal for about fifteen people, read her newspaper on Sundays and have a cup of coffee. I would later come to realize it was pent up trauma. Her silence was loud! As I recall, I've never heard my grandmother acknowledge her feelings. She was always available to help others acknowledge theirs. The things that are revealed when you're healing. As I reflect on my life, I am faced with the reflections of the lives that surrounded me.

Some of my fondest memories of my granny would be sitting on our front porch and talking to her about why I'd gotten suspended from school and how it made my mother feel. I remember those days when the house would be silent and I'd sneak in her bedroom to play in her perfumes, lotions and admire her baubles and fancy dresses she'd buy from Dillard's or from the boosters that would bring stolen merchandise by the house for her to peruse and purchase. I was there for it, honey! Our rides to Barnett Bank as she made her financial transactions of checking and saving while I played my little game of "bank" in the waiting area. Now "Bank" was a game that I made up in my head where I would act like I was the bank clerk and the greeter at the same time. If you don't understand, ask me about it when I'm interviewed about The Chronicles of S.H.E.

Shadows

My face is no longer familiar; my eyes do not show the passion they once inspired; I am not what you remember. I am forgotten…my face is no longer familiar.

Your touch makes me nervous. Your gaze is not sexy, it's frightening. Your love making molests me, I'm tired! You are a stranger…You are no longer familiar.

My sun no longer rises northeast; the moon no longer lights my night. I am alone. This house has made me blue, I'm so sick of you; in my heart I have a home and it's always with me. This place is no longer familiar.

Open my eyes, open my eyes, o'pen my eyes and to my surprise standing there in your miraculous glory, Moon light shining brightening my night; enhancing my soul. Words of love flowed from your mouth to my inner most emotions. Spirits within yelling intercourse! You're now a part of me and this is so familiar.

In my mind, like yesterday, recurrences of you, these beautiful feelings, hurt and despair…I am reminded of you, but…with a different voice.

O' how I long to reach you, to show you I understand you, to give you peace; to allow you sweet release…no struggle no pain. Why can't you see I am you! I love me loving you.

CHAPTER 3

By time I was thirteen; nothing really interesting happened in my life. By now, I'd become the nightmare; no one said a word to me out of the way. My fist was hard and fast and my ability to find a weapon was nothing sort of assassinating. That didn't stop the bullying though; but at least I'd learned how to not only stand up for myself but to also protect myself. That girl Princess was truly not Princess by definition at this point. I'd become "Napéphečą Nážiŋ Wiŋ," which translate from Lakota to English as *Stands with a Fist*! Ok, I know ya'll have seen the movie *Dances with Wolves?*"

There was one incident in the house when I'd stabbed my cousin Snookie in his arm five times for picking on me in front of my friend who had become his girlfriend. I was sitting in the den area of my granny's house watching the sitcom *Family Matters*. Snookie and Towanna comes walking in the room loud and all kissy face. I'd politely asked them to be a little quieter because I was trying to watch television. Well, maybe I wasn't as polite as I'd thought… but oh well. From there Snookie started making fun of my hair which had fallen out due to untreated home relaxers. He made fun of my clothes and then kicked me in my back. I got up and walked to the kitchen. I opened the flatware drawer and pulled out a steak knife. Then, marched my little self-back in the den and as he was kissing Towanna; I positioned the steak knife in my right hand and went to work on his arm. Towanna scurried to the side of the sofa and screamed, "Snookie she got a knife." Snookie, yelped in pain but stood up and punched me in my face. I didn't care; I was ready for him. But, Towanna was like "let's go to my house Snookie." They left and I finished watching my television show. Typical day and moving on.

Anyhow, things started to shift a bit once my mother returned home from rehab and got a job with Bank of America and marrying my stepfather, John. John was in the U.S. Navy; I am not sure of his rank, but what I do know is our lives changed drastically. My mom was no longer a single-mother; although she was still married to my dad. (That's another topic in itself.) There was more than one income coming into our home so of course life had gotten better for us. My now parents decided that the family needed a change and my stepdad was up for relocation. There was a choice between Scotland and Beltsville, Maryland. My parents chose the latter.

Moving to Maryland was a total game-changer for a girl like me. I mean back then I wasn't quite girly; I was more tom-boyish, a little dainty and a lot rugged. The women in my family are women in every sense of the word but they're ruthless. The young men in the family are highly intelligent but they're quite dangerous. The older men in my family were just that men; country salt to the earth; men.

It was a bit difficult coming to terms with our new residence and way of life. Again, I was never good at making friends; my younger brother was the more charismatic of the two of us. My mom was so over the top… hindsight I can understand why. My mother was finally happy to be able to give her children a safe environment in which to learn discover and grow. She'd enrolled us both into our respective schools; me being in the 8th grade, had to attend Buck Lodge Middle School located in Prince Georges County (PG County). My goodness; what a culture shock!

I'd attended school with different races but for the most part we were all from the same neighborhood. I was still socially awkward. Buck Lodge was truly a Mecca of culture for me at that time. I was exposed to different ethnic groups, real hip-hop, and real Latin American culture. I was faced with the understanding of "quasi-Northern" urban cultural dynamics as oppose to my Florida Southern swag. I met peers from Africa… yesssss AFRICA. Now, I've had friends from Africa living in my childhood neighborhood in Jacksonville, but they were more American than I was. I heard languages that set my ears on fire. I heard music that resonated with my soul… I just didn't understand how it all would play a part in my life.

I remember the first time I entered a classroom at Buck Lodge. Oh boy, what a mess. I felt like I was dressed to the nines. I'd gone to the Gateway Flea Market and had a pair of shorts engraved with my name on them before we left Florida. I'd bought me a fresh Charlotte Hornets shirt and a fresh pair of Charles Barkley's. I'd put my hair up in the tightest ponytail and my edges were laid honey. Needless to say, I was ready…so I'd thought. Honey, we I got to the school and looked around I knew that I was not dressed "right." Nevertheless, I stepped foot into my first class; and from there it was a real shit show.

First, the teacher didn't even greet me; he just motioned for me to find a seat. I stood at the door looking around the trying to find the nearest yet most secluded seat in the room. Just then, a young boy name Erin (Earl) screamed across the room; "Why you carrying me YO?!" I had no idea who he was talking to nor did I understand his meaning. I continued to stand there looking for a seat…awkward because now everyone in class was looking at me including the damn teacher. By this time, Erin (Earl) made his way to his feet and walking in my direction shouting; "Why you carrying me YO?" I responded, "What are talking about I haven't even picked you up Dawg?" The class was like, "Ooooooo she called you a dog." I was oh ok here we go. I guess Erin (Earl) was like the head honcho at the school. At this point, he was close to me and shouting, "wait until class is over Imma get my girl Vanessa to beat your ass." Now like I said, I was a bit rugged. I flat out told him; "Dawg, don't wait for your girl let's get it nigga!" He started shouting, "You lucky I don't hit girls." Now that's funny, back then I didn't consider myself to be a girl; I was just Princess.

By now, the bell had rang to end class and here I am walking through the hallway searching for my next class and all I hear is female voices chattering about the new girl and what type of ass whooping I was about to catch. I was a bit nervous to be honest but my momma told me to stay ready for whatever and that's what I did. I turned around and asked the group; "Now, who gone beat my ass." They started talking about my outfit; of course. My hair was not up to their standard and that became the focal point... yet no one stepped to me in any way. I repeated my previous question, "Now who gonna beat my ass, again?" By this time, Erin (Earl) walked up grabbed Vanessa's hand and guided her to her next class. I stood there; still ready for whatever. This cool chick walked up to me and said, "Hey! My name Suehail...I'm from Florida too...Broward County-Overtown." I had no clue what Broward County and Overtown was but I was like what's up Dawg.

We chilled and then she introduced me to a few other real cool chicks and we just all vibed. Needless to say, I went home and vowed that I would never step foot back into that school again. My parents questioned why and I emotionally explained to them that I had to change my dress code ASAP. Boy, the issues of a drama teen. My stepdad looked at my momma and said; "Cynt, let's take these kids shopping. I told you they were going to need new clothes." My momma laughed... she was a bit old fashioned, yet she agreed. The next day at school was a bit better. I still never understood why Erin came at me so hard... but I am glad that I reciprocated his energy or else I would have been bullied the remainder of the school year.

It was the summer of '94, 8th grade graduation time. I was glad to be entering high school but not in Maryland. I still had no friends in my neighborhood and my little brother was starting to make me jealous of his social life. How pathetic is that? Not as pathetic as your mom going out making friends for you and then bringing them to the house for you to meet. OMG! The horror; right? In my bedroom lying across my bed reading a book and listening to Anita Baker's song "*I Apologize*" on the radio and in walks my mother. This woman had a smile on her face the lit up the atmosphere yet in a very coy tone she says, "What'cha doing? Get up and come out in the living room; I want you to meet some people." I was confused but I got up any way. As I gathered myself, I followed my mother's lead into the living room and there stood two girls about my age dressed in long skirts and blouses. In my head I asked myself, "Who are these people," as if I could answer. My mom with that same smile on her face says, "Princess, this is Dominique and Catherine." I said the usual hello and they excitingly and simultaneously spoke, "Hello!" Oh Gosh!

Dominique and Catherine were neighbors in our building as we lived in Powder Mill. They were pretty cool and Dominique had a voice of an angel. But they were not my cup of tea as their family were devoted Jehovah's Witnesses and I didn't understand the dynamic at the time. Especially coming from the household I grew up in. Needless to say, I was quite nostalgic as I'd forgot to mention that I had obtained a little boyfriend before leaving Jacksonville. Yep, Anthony "Lil Tony" Campbell. Whew! Lil Tony and I met on a three-way phone call with mutual friends.

So, there was this girl named Erinna that moved to Atlantic Beach. Erinna had a twin brother named Erin who tragically passed away after we all had met. Erinna was from Jacksonville's Northside over off of Moncrief Road. Erinna a bit awkward as her name but she was nice all the same. Anyway, Erinna had a boyfriend named Lil Tony and he had a friend named Carlos. She was to hook me up with Carlos but there was no way we could travel to the Northside from the Beaches without our parents knowing; we decided to call one another and then each of us would call one of the guys.

Well, we all ended up on the phone call and we just chatted away. Needless to say, I was drawn in by Lil Tony's southern Duval County twang in his voice. So after caking on the phone with these folks for about 2 hours my grandmother noticed that I was on the phone and commenced to yelling, "Princess, get off the phone." I reluctantly said goodbye to the group and hung up. The next day, I received a call from Lil Tony! I was so nervous and giddy. I had to get on the phone with long cord (if you know, you know) and huddle up in my room so I could talk to Lil Tony. His first words to me were, "So what's up." That lil' bit right there sent me swinging ya hear me. Moving on, Lil Tony and I talked on the phone with one another for hours that developed into years without ever physically laying eyes on one another.

After the move to Maryland, Lil' Tony and I became loving pen pals. I would write to see him and send him pictures of myself in my new environment. I would tell him all about my days and nights. I shared every experience with him. He would send me encouraging words that would soothe me and give meaning to facing another day. He sent me a card once that read, "Without you, something's missing from my corner of the world." The game changed once I found out how to make long-distance calls. Oooowwweee the trouble I got into once my parents got the phone bills that I had been hiding each month.

Ok, now back to my teenage life in Maryland, after meeting Dominique and Catherine I'd decided to get up out of my room and go check out the neighborhood. This of course, pleased my mom. I'd equipped my hip with my walkman locked and loaded Aaliyah's *Age Ain't Nothing But A Number* CD, put on my headphones and went for a walk. I continued this same pattern for about three days switching between Aaliyah and Brandy until I was approached by a group of girls my age... Cora, Nala, Pooh and Penny. I didn't know what they wanted but I slowly removed my headphones as the music continued to play. I asked them what they wanted and then Cora asked if I was new out there. I replied with yes and that my family had recently moved in. They asked what school I went to; which at that time I was a student at High Point as I'd just entered the 9th grade. I didn't really care for High Point outside of my French and Civics classes. At any rate, I'd met my friends for life... Cora, Nala, Pooh and Penny. I was slowly introduced to more teens in the neighborhood which was pretty cool. We were a band of misfits.

Later, I met this awesome ball of exceptional talent, that stood 5'4" and full of life; Tomeka! Tomeka was my girl. She knew all of the latest dances and could move just like Janet Jackson. I admired her. Tomeka inhabited a free spirited approach to life and dare devilish attitude but all in good fun. I then met the Trinidadian bombshell, Jah'tina! These chicas taught me some moves ya' heard. I started to shed that Tomboyish swag and slid into a divine feminine, just kick it, but get out of my face girlish strut. I liked it there.

I would spend time at Tomeka's while her mother was at work and we would do chores and watch videos as we danced the day away. If I were not at Tomeka's I would visit Jah'tina's house where her mother would be blaring sounds of Calypso and Soca. The rooms were filled with incense and Caribbean spices. Now, being from Florida, reggae music was familiar but to experience reggae music is a different thing. I remember one time while I was visiting Jah'tina's, her mom was playing this song *Poom Poom Shorts* by Red Fox and Screechie Dan. Jah'tina and her mother were dancing and it looked so fun. I stood there happily watching the two of them cut the rug when her mother grabbed my hand while saying in a thick Trini accent, "Come now gal." I was like I don't know how to do all of that. Her mother says to me, "Whine your hips honey, come on now gal!" I started to mimic what I was seeing and I guess I wasn't quite hitting it. Needless to say, I got a lesson that day that would later come in handy.

My stepdad had applied for military housing which afforded us the opportunity to make residence on Fort Meade's military base which was approximately 45 minutes from Powder Mill. Yeah, we had to move. The move was bittersweet but I didn't mind much as I'd gotten a new lease on life. Once we moved to Fort Meade, I continued my routine which entailed my walkman but this time instead Aaliyah and Brandy I was now listening to Northeast Groovers, Rare Essence and all of that good Washington D.C. Go-Go music. I would walk the confines of our cul-de-sac listening to my beats. Until, one day my mom approached me telling me that it was time to enroll into school.

So now I'm transferring from High Point High School to Fort Meade High School. The schools were totally different especially with Meade being on a military base that accepted students that were not military children. The school structure was different, the dress code was different, the accents of the people were different... it was different. Prince George's County Maryland was more D.C. while Fort Meade was in Anne Arundel County which was more Baltimore; well at least that was my reasonable deduction of the two. The music and fashion styles were distinctive. I feel in love with both! Not sure if you've picked up on the theme here; I used music as a way to drown out the world and engulfed myself into the artistry of it all.

My time on Fort Meade were the best of times and the worst of times. Up to this time, I'd evolved into a social introvert. What is a social introvert, you ask? A social introvert is an introvert who enjoys socializing with others. They may prefer to spend time alone or in small groups, and may find large social gatherings draining. Social introverts may still prefer more meaningful interactions with close friends than the average introvert. I was able to make friends a lot easier than ever before in my life. Also, military children living on a military base are more equipped to socialize with one another as they may have moved around more often than other children in civilian households. While my brother and I didn't grow up in a military household, our lives prepared us for this as we'd moved around quite a bit ourselves. And my experiences in Powder Mill, Silver Creek, Atlantic Beach and Jax Beach taught me a few things; if I do say so myself.

Upon meeting my new found friend girls Chunda, Mello, Bernice, Sunshine, Zia, Spice, Ray, June-Bug, and Chainy to name a few or dare I say the lot; I let my hair down for the first time in my life. The E.P.

Crew is was what we'd crowned ourselves; named after the infamous Ernie Pyle Court which was the name of the street that connected us all. We all would get together and talk the day away, reminiscing of our hometowns and the music that connected us all as we are hailed from varying parts of the South. Listening to one another's stories of what the day made and how we were ready for the world. By this time, my distance romance with Lil' Tony had fizzled. Yet, he remains in my heart still.

School days were a little tough for me as I never did very well in school; hell I couldn't complete a full week of school without being suspended, expelled, or in detention since the 3rd grade. I don't know why I'd never failed a grade; I guess I was a good test taker. I showed very little interest in my classes with the exception of Art, Biology and History. English came natural as I've been an avid reader. I simply dreaded sitting in a classroom for the allotted time; I wanted to move on to next thing. Now they have a term for that which is ADD (attention-deficit disorder). I wish my mom had known about this; I'm sure she would wish she'd known as well.

In Maryland, I didn't get into much trouble in school as I'd done in Florida. I presume the change in environment did me some good. I can definitely say I matured once we'd relocated. We didn't have poisonous venom of dysfunction in our home. However, sometimes old habits are hard to shake. I still possessed unresolved anger issues, violent tendencies, and a strong sense of damn or be damned which I let loose on my siblings and anyone else that I felt stepped out of line with me. Keep reading; there's more that will bring all of this tea about me together for a refreshing rock in a chair on the porch at sunset.

CHAPTER 4

Here we are back in Jacksonville, Florida with "the family." This time, things were different. My mother had her confidence back which resembled the "Cynt" that had taught my brother and I to read at the age of three. The mother who deemed our house a haven of Black Empowerment and learning. Our home consisted of Encyclopedia written by Black American authors; similar to Africana: The Encyclopedia of The African and African-American Experience 5-Volume Set. My *Mother* was stronger, sober… she was alive.

I, myself, had relinquished my tomboyish antics. My bosom at the ripe age were firm fitting for a 36c bra. I stood 5'6" with a weight of 125lbs; can you say <u>Brick House!</u> Well, that's what I'd thought. My time in Maryland had given me the confidence to embrace the natural birthed brilliance of wearing my natural hair; which I'd worn in a sleek radiant crop that accented my curl patterns. My chocolate skin had been kissed by the sun and bathe with the hidden gem of Black Soap. The flowers in my mind had been watered by the mathematics of day as presented by the musical geniuses of the *Wu-Tang Clan's 36 Chambers*. Oh dare I mention how my soul had experienced the teaching of the Five Percent Nation, The Nation of Islam, Judaism and Buddhism. My soul radiated… *Most High!*

The fall came slowly and painfully as experiences came to teach me lessons that I could never learn in a book!

After getting pregnant at seventeen years old and having my baby girl at the age of eighteen years old; life became sort of a blur. I moved in with my daughter's father who really didn't want me there but I was what they called "In House Pussy." Yes, I said it…It distinctly meant that my daughter's father had access to my body at his will since we lived in the same home. I felt like I was being raped every time he touched me; but where would I go? I couldn't go home; nobody wanted me there; at least that's the way it seemed at the time.

Childhood traumas came flooding back like the mighty Mississippi River.

While I'd just had my eighteenth birthday, Perry; my daughter's father was twenty-three years old. I was always told that I should date men older; my family considered me to be quite "mature" for my age. I later found out what they meant by that. I physically developed earlier than my peers and I'd been what they considered "exposed," "touched," to say it blatantly raped. So, I dated Perry, made a child with Perry and later moved in with Perry. People always made fun of how Ike Turner beat Tina Turner but no one would have guessed that Ike couldn't hold a candle to Perry. He'd beat me for overcooking the food. "He'd hit me because I was too smart. He'd hit me because I... was me.

I couldn't go home at this point if I'd wanted to. My mother was hospitalized for a brain aneurysm. She'd had surgery and survived but she was on the road to recovery. My family pretty much banished me from coming home... my Aunt Pamela lied to my stepfather about my daughter's dad staying over to the house which simply wasn't true. No one asked me the truth so my stepdad kicked me out. Phase-three of self-destruction...

This question would always linger in the back of my subconscious; "Who can I run to?" Seriously, who could I turn to in my desperate hour? Once my mother was released from the hospital from having recovered from a Neurological surgery that removed an aneurysm, she sent for me. I was little relieved but I was also nervous as I didn't quite know what to expect.

I would guess that I chose to move back home as that trauma there was more familiar than what I was currently experiencing. The lessor of two evils. While I definitely didn't realize that I was traumatized then; I knew that I wouldn't have to fight or be beaten like that if I went back to my momma house who was then living in my grandmother's house.

Perry and I lived on the Northside of Jacksonville just off of Moncrief Road and Myrtle Avenue. I was sitting on the bed in our room watching some random show thinking about how scared I was going to be when it got dark while Perry was at work and I would be in the house alone. As I was contemplating how I would escape the apartment if someone broke in; I heard a knock at the front door.

It was still daylight so I shimmied myself out of bed; by this time I was about five months into my pregnancy. I walked slowly to the door shouting, "Who is it?" The voice coming from the other side of the door was quite refreshing. It was my cousin, Kamryn. Happy to hear her voice, I put a little rush in my steps towards the door. As I opened the door, I could smell her perfume as usual it hid the faint smells of marijuana. Be that as it may, I was happy to see my cousin.

As I opened the door, Kamryn pushed her way through the front door while greeting me as well as assessing my living conditions. Kamryn asked, "What you doing in here?" "Why is it so dark in here," she asked. I passively responded, "Nothing, just sitting here watching t.v." She says to me, "Get dressed your momma is out of the hospital and she wants to see you." Inside I cried on the outside I was a little apprehensive as I didn't know what to expect. I was no longer her little girl any more as there I stood bare foot, nappy headed and five months pregnant. I went into my room and started to dress myself; however, nothing seemed suitable to wear. I decided to put on a grey Tommy Hilfiger dress that Perry had stolen during one of his many smash and grab escapades in Georgia.

I'd combed my short hair down to be as styled as it could be as it had not been properly treated in months. We walked out of the door; I was unable to lock the door as I didn't have a key.

Kamryn asked, "Why you ain't lock the door, Princess?" I told her that I didn't have a key to lock the door; that Perry just assumes that I am not going anywhere. Perry's assumption was typically correct as I was somewhat afraid to leave out of the house due to the nature of the neighborhood and I didn't have my own money.

Kamryn and I drove silently to my grandmother's house which is where I would find my momma waiting for me. I slowly exited the vehicle due to my state of being as well as apprehension. As I walked through the door my heart hit the floor as soon as my eyes met the eyes of my mother. My momma was not her best self but she stood up to greet and embrace me with tears in her eyes. The hug she gave me was one asking, "What has happened to my baby?" I embraced her but I felt an enormous amount of anger brewing in my soul as she asked me where I'd been and why I'd left home. I didn't want to hurt her so I kept the truth to myself.

The truth is, when I became pregnant I was still living at home. After my mom was admitted into the hospital for the aneurysm, I'd invited my baby's daddy sister, Jessica, over to braid my hair since I was still considered a child and could not make the decision to stay out late. Jessica came over and braided my hair into Mircobraids; it took forever. Hours had gone by and just as she finished I noticed that Jessica was too tired to drive home; it was already 1:00AM. I'd called my momma's hospital room and asked her if Jessica could stay; my mom said yes.

Later that morning, my Aunt Pamela stopped by for whatever reason and saw that Jessica was asleep on the sofa. I guess her seeing that, she assumed whatever…I can't tell you what she was thinking but I can tell you what she did. She waited until my stepdad came home from work and told him that I'd had my baby's daddy sleeping over and that it was time for me to go since I was the one that was stressing my momma out which ultimately put my momma in the hospital with the aneurysm. Wow, how awful is that? My stepdad listened to her and put me out. That twisted deed turned my life upside down. I'd dropped out of school being a child and pregnant. I was not prepared for the hardships that I was facing and about to face.

Nevertheless, after visiting with my mom and family, I was convinced to move back home; into my grandmother's home. It was cool at first as my grandparents had turned the den area of the home into my bedroom. The atmosphere was very familiar as that was the house that I'd grew up in as a child, yet things were very different. My little brother, who was just two years younger than I, was now selling and doing drugs with a baby on the way too. The effects of substance abuse lingered heavily in the atmosphere, but it was home… the lesser of two evils.

CHAPTER 5

Catching the evening bus from school was always refreshing as it meant that I was only within moments of indulging in my chocolate donuts my grandmother would stop and get me from Dunkin Donuts; they were my absolute favorite. I can taste them now. One particular ride home with always stand out in my mind, the late afternoon of October 9, 1998, it was a Friday. School had just let out and I'd made my way to my bus. I sat in the front seat to the right as it was required considering my "condition." The ride started off as our typical ride home; one bus stop after the next and a group of kids would make their way down the stairs existing the bus. Well, our driver got distracted and almost missed someone's stop; the bus driver slammed on breaks.

I made my way home after reaching my stop. As I walked into the door two of my aunts were there with a few of their children. One of my aunts was in the kitchen frying chicken, making pork and beans with rice with the infamous household Kool-Aid. As the southern aromas filled the home, the rising levels in my hormones had caused my olfactory senses to heighten which caused a wanting to my taste buds. Simply put I wanted some chicken so bad! I knew that I would have to wait for the smaller children to eat before I was presented with the opportunity to dig in so I moved on to my room. I unloaded my backpack onto my bed and plopped down with exhaustion.

As I grabbed the television remote control, one of my lil' cousins came barging into my room while exclaiming in our southern Florida twang, "Princess, my momma said come here!"

"Ok, go tell her I'm coming."

I sighed heavily and stood from my bed. Slipped on my house shoes and walked towards the kitchen. My aunt heard me coming and side eyed me while asking if I were hungry.

"Of course!" I stated.

"Well get yourself a plate and get your fill. You know you gotta feed that baby."

I replied, "Yes ma'am," with a smile on my face.

I walked into the dining area, went into the cupboard and grabbed one of my grandmother's Pyrex Blue Ring Vintage Retro plates along with a Flat Iced Tea Wexford glass for my Kool-Aid. It was on from there; if you know, you know. If not, I commenced to fixing my plate, loading it with chicken and a spread of buttery white rice while mounting a heap of pork and beans on top of my rice with two tablespoons of sugar; grub.

After I demolished my dinner, I had an immediate feeling of *the itis*. A normal feeling of drowsiness or lassitude after eating a meal is how you would define *the itis*. Some would call this an after-dinner dip. I wanted to be left alone and bask in the ambiance of hunger satisfaction. Upon that feeling, I'd decided to bathe. A hot meal and hot shower was all pregnant teen girl would need.

I gathered my bath kit which consisted of my drying towel, wash cloth, face cloth, Irish Spring soap, Noxzema, shower shoes and my previous Jergens lotion. I'd entered my grandparent's bedroom which led into a shared shower which was the master bathroom as the plumbing for the bathtub in the guest bathroom wasn't working. Come to think of it; I cannot recall a time that the plumbing for the bathtub in the guest bathroom ever working...*hmmm*.

Moving on; I'd turned on the hot water of the shower. As I waited for the temperature of the water to rise, I peeked in mirror to give myself the once over. Aware that I am pregnant but unaware that there's an actual life growing inside of me. Of course, I knew that I was carrying a child. I was actually looking at how much my stomach had grown. That very moment, I'd felt this strange internal movement all while knowing that it was my baby girl. Not aware of the signs!

Testing the water temperature with my hand, I deduced that the shower was just right for me. I stepped into the shower with thoughts of what my daughter would like. Her father while scrawny was quite cute. Then my mind drifted to Lil' Tony as I recalled a baby picture of himself that he'd share with me. He was so adorable. So as I washed, I also prayed and asked God above to bless my child with the features which combined her father's likeness along with the hair and gorgeousness of Lil' Tony's baby photo. I prayed to God to not allow my daughter to look anything like me. I didn't want her to inherit my dark skin, the gap between my front top teeth… *"God, please just don't her look like me!"* Guess, you can tell by that, my self-esteem was in toilet.

After my pleading prayer, I was done washing up. I stepped from the shower, grabbed my Jergens to lotion my body while damp (see below for reasons why).

Applying lotion right after a shower

- *Moisturizes skin: When skin is wet, it's more permeable to moisture. This helps lock in moisture and prevent dryness.*
- *Helps skin absorb ingredients: Applying lotion to damp skin allows the skin to better absorb the main ingredients in the product.*

I'd applied the lotion liberally to my damp warm skin. However, I could not shake that strange internal movement. I'd brushed it off mentally, accepting the fact that it was my baby making herself comfortable. Boy, was I wrong! As I leaned over to grab my undergarments and just as I'd reached forward, a trickle of water leaked from my vagina.

I'd thought to myself *Girl, I know you ain't peeing*, puzzled.

Just then my grandmother had come home from and entered her bedroom and found me standing there, naked and peeing. What a sight, huh?

Facing my grandmother standing at her room's door, I burst with laughter while apologizing to her for pissing on her floor and assured her that I would clean the mess. My granny laughed right back at me.

Excitingly my granny says, *"Cynt, it's time! This girl finna have a baby!"*

I froze.

"I'm about to have a baby?"

I heard my mother's from the far part of the house. *"Awww shit damn, I just got home from work!"*

My grandmother changed from her work clothing into something more comfortable. My mother made a call to someone telling them that I was now in labor. Once the phone line cleared, I called Perry to explain to that I was in labor. Of course he didn't believe me as ironically his birthday was the day before, October 9th. I didn't bother to mince words with him, so I hung and proceeded to my room.

Here I am, standing in the middle of my makeshift bedroom, glancing at the baby's bassinet which was given to me by one of my godmother's. I walked over to ensure that I'd sanitized it properly during my nesting phase. I glanced up to reflect on how I'd decorated the room which the colorful letters of the alphabet and the coinciding limericks. I went over to bed and sat at the edge of it while rubbing my tummy and ensuring my baby that I was her mom all while trying to convince I was ready to be her mom. I reached over to grasp her Winnie-Pooh diaper in which I'd prepared weeks ago as instructed by my Lamaze instructor. I was given a birthing preparation book during one of my Lamaze classes; I made sure that I had that book inside of the baby's bag.

As I sat at the edge of my bed, holding my stomach with one hand and gripping the baby's bag; my cousin Laiana barged in.

"Get up! Me and Ricky here to take you to the hospital."

"Ok, I need to call the hospital" That's what my doctor instructed me to do and so did my Lamaze instructor.

"Girl, if you don't come here."

"Laiana, can she even stand-up?" asked Ricky.

"Yeah, she's sitting here like ain't nothing happening."

"Ya'll know Princess crazy child," says my momma.

While *the family* proceeded with their commentary, I made my way off of the bed while reciting Psalms 23:1-6. And it reads according to the King James Version of The Bible,

Psalm 23:1–6

1 The Lord is my shepherd; I shall not want.

2 He maketh me to lie down in green pastures: he leadeth me beside the still waters.

3 He restoreth my soul: he leadeth me in the paths of righteousness for his name's sake.

4 Yea, though I walk through the valley of the shadow of death, I will fear no evil: for thou art with me; thy rod and thy staff they comfort me.

5 Thou preparest a table before me in the presence of mine enemies: thou anointest my head with oil; my cup runneth over.

6 Surely goodness and mercy shall follow me all the days of my life: and I will dwell in the house of the Lord forever.

CHAPTER 6

During my pregnancy, I'd made a vow that my daughter would have a different upbringing than I, which began with a relationship with the Lord God. I'd read somewhere that babies are learning while in the womb. Whatever you read, learn, and experience, the baby also reads, learns and experiences. Each day after completing my homework, I would turn the radio station to the AM's Classical channel. I'd lay across my bed with my grandmother's devotional teaching bible and begin to read The Book of Psalms of which I found comfort. I would also force myself to read my Math book's lesson outlines and examples. I didn't understand it but I'd hoped that she did. Well at least she would have the exposure. A little hint, it worked too. My daughter was an honor student all through school in spite of dyslexia she'd inherited from her father.

I'd made my way to Laiana and Ricky's SUV, loaded myself into the back cabin. I rolled my window down to ask Josie if my hair was ok. You can't go to the hospital to have a baby looking crazy. Well, so I was told. Josie confirmed and explained to me that having my baby wouldn't be so bad. She would know, especially since she'd only had her daughter two months prior. Mind you, Josie and I are the same age. Her birthing experience was different as she required a C-section. I prayed that I would not have that experience.

Rickey was the driver while Laiana coached the both of us from the passenger's seat. I didn't feel any pain which caused the two to panic which heightened the anxiety. I must say that I'd gotten a nice chuckle from the drama of it. Rickey looked at me through the rear-view mirror.

"*Girl, you alright back there?*" Rickey asked.

I remained silent as I focused my thoughts on the words blaring inside; *it's time.*

It's time? While understanding exactly what that'd meant; I was puzzled. You see, I was told that I would never be able to have children due to the trauma that I'd experienced as a young child. I was molested and my body had been severely damaged from the inside. This caused major affects to my reproductive health. Hence, I couldn't children.

No one ever asked how I'd gotten pregnant. I guess that wouldn't be a question to ask since we all know how it happens. But what happened to me? I'd met a guy at a nightclub while out with a childhood friend. Don't ask why I was in a nightclub at 17 years old; just know I was in there. I was in there and having a ball. The music blared erotic South Florida tunes and I was P-Popping on a handstand. The dance floor was lit!

Well, after all of my pop lock and dropping, I'd needed a drink. While I didn't drink alcohol at the time, I went over to the bar and requested a Tahitian Treat. Don't laugh; yes, I wanted a Tahitian Treat and asked for it. The bartender gave me the once over and provided me with my request. I'd stepped out of the line with my Tahitian Treat in hand and commenced to quench my thirst. While standing with my back against the wall basking in the ambiance of the club; this guy walked over to me. Intrigued by what he'd saw; which was me, he approached me and asked my name.

My response was something fake of course; who gives out their real name in the club? He in turned introduced himself and gestured a toast as he too had a Tahitian Treat. We both got a good laugh at that. The club was closing and I'd began to make my way to the front door. I'd given the guy my telephone number and asked him to call me after 4 pm as I would be home from school at that time. I'd guess that prompted him to ask my age. I told him that I was seventeen.

He wanted to walk me to my car. I was a little apprehensive but he'd seem harmless. As we walked towards the car, the guy asked me if it was okay for us to stop by his car for a moment. I didn't question why; and walked over to his car with him. Why did I do that? Once we got to his vehicle, the look in his eyes changed. He'd become what I identified as at the time, strange.

"My cousins might be looking for me. I'd better go."

"No, just wait a minute. I'm going to walk you to your car."

I attempted to walk away. But he aggressively grabbed my arm and poked me in the side with a knife.

"Don't move and don't scream!" He whispered in my ears.

The back car door was already opened as he done so when we first approached the vehicle. He'd said that he needed grab something which was why we went walked to his car in the first place. How dumb of me, right? To have trusted a whole stranger all because we shared a moment over Tahitian Treat.

"Get in the car." He said with force.

"No, I am not getting in there." "Let me go, nigga!"

I'd felt the knife penetrate my flesh. I could feel my warm blood trickle down my lower abdomen. I got in car.

After he was done, he lifted himself off of me while fixing his pants. The silence was thick.

"Are you okay?" He asked.

I mumbled, "ummhmm…" and sighed.

Why did I get in the car? Why didn't I fight?

I made my way out of his vehicle and slowly made my way to cousin's car where she was waiting for me.

"Girl, where the hell have you been?" She yelled.

"Nowhere, I just wanna go home."

That guy was Perry.

It's time! We'd made it to the hospital. Rickey abruptly pulled into the ER entrance and slammed on brakes. You could hear the rubber burning as the SUV came to an immediate halt.

"Babe, Imma go get her a wheelchair. Princess stay in the car!" Rickey shouted as he hopped out of the driver's seat

"Princess, just breathe okay. Breathe." Laiana commanded.

I understood the rush of labor and all. However, I wasn't experiencing any pain and I was calm as a cucumber. I only wondered what would my baby look and if I was going to be a good mom. I'd actually thought that I was prepared. I was quite embarrassed by the actions of Rickey and Laiana because I felt they were being overly dramatic.

Rickey quickly made his way back to the SUV with the wheelchair to find that I'd already existed standing and waiting. I sat down in the wheelchair while Rickey swiftly pushed me into the ER's waiting area. I was trying to explain to the two neurotics that we were in the wrong area. They couldn't hear me over their panic of me being in labor.

Laiana went over to the check-in counter of the emergency room.

"My lil' cousin is having a baby. Somebody need to do something now!"

"Where is she?" The woman at the check-in counter asked.

"She's over there in that wheelchair." Laiana said while pointing in my direction.

"Has her water broke?" The check-in woman asked in a relaxed tone.

"Yeah, well not really but yeah!" Laiana said.

Just then, a gush of water from my body fell to the floor. Oh gosh, I was truly embarrassed. I put my hands over my face with shame. I could hear the chatter from the people in the crowded emergency room.

"Get that girl some help!" A woman shouted.

"She's about to have that baby." Exclaimed another woman with a raspy voice.

The check-in counter lady came rushing over to me.

"You ready, baby?" She asked.

I nodded my head to confirm.

Here I am being wheeled around the hospital on my way to Labor and Delivery.

CHAPTER 7

Labor and Delivery

I was assigned to a room for monitoring. I was connected to an ultrasound device which monitored my baby's heartbeat. The rapid thuds soothe me like the ocean. A nurse walked in smiling with a puzzled look on her face. She greeted me as she walked closer to my bedside.

"Baby, how are you doing? Are you thirsty?" The nurse asked.

"Yes, ma'am."

"Let me check your vitals and then I'll get you some ice chips."

"Yes, ma'am."

The nurse checked my vital signs; you know blood pressure, pulse and temperature to ensure they were in normal range. I guess all was good as she put away her stethoscope and walked towards the door. Just as she made it to the door the nurse took a glance at the tocodynamometer which printed out paper to show my contractions.

"Baby, do you feel that?

I replied, "What?"

"Those contractions." The nurse stated.

"No, ma'am."

The nurse left my room with a look of confusion.

Just as soon as the nurse left the room different family members began to enter. All of them with smiles of joy and laughter. Each of them as they entered expressed their happiness as well as concern for me. It brought me great joy to see and talk with each of them.

"Princess, cuz you good?" Asked my cousin Michael.

Smiling, I replied, "Yeah. I'm good."

"Could someone hand me my baby bag, please?"

My cousin Michael handed me the baby bag. I pulled out an Apple flavored Blow Pop.

"Cuz, you want candy right now?"

"Yes, my labor and delivery coach told me that this would be good to have just in case I experienced dry mouth."

"Man, what?" Michael asked in dismay.

Just then the nurse walked in to room and made her way over to the tocodynamometer device. Her eyes widened as she took in the results. Her feet stepped back and she turned in an about face motion. Gingerly making her way to the door, the nurse asked everyone to leave. No one gave her any pushback; they made their way out of the door. I could hear soft whispers, "It must be time."

I latched on to my Blow Pop whilst eating my ice chips. The sounds of the ultrasound machine and an episode from "The Young and Restless" filled my room. I was coolin'. The nurse walks back into my room this time accompanied by the doctor. The nurse smiled pleasantly as the doctor introduced himself. This time, the doctor checked my vitals and asked how I was feeling. I'd felt great; very relaxed.

"Nurse, how far apart are those contractions?" The doctor asked the nurse.

"3 minutes, doctor. The nurse replied.

At this point, the doctor was nearing the wash sink. Turning on the water, the doctor looked over at me as he commenced to washing his hands. The nurse stepped out and came back with the delivery team.

"Now, you're going to feel a little bit of pressure." The doctor warned as he placed one hand on my belly and used the other to position his finger inside my cervix. He was checking for dilation stages. The doctor pushed back and removed his gloves. He spoke with the delivery team game planning their next moves as I laid there watching television.

"Doctor, I can see the head!" One nurse exclaimed.

"Welp, no time for all of that. Looks like we have an impatient baby." The doctor jokingly stated.

A nurse provided him with a new set of latex gloves.

"It's time to push. Now when I tell you, start pushing."

"Okay." I said while nodding my head.

The nurse took my Blow Pop.

"You're going to okay, baby girl." The nurse's comforting words reassured me that all would be well.

"Pushhhhh"

I pushed.

"Pushhhhh"

I pushed.

"Ok, now just one more big push."

"Push, Push, Push, Push…" The doctor rapidly repeated.

I pushed as hard as I could.

"We have a baby girl!" The nurse spoke with excitement. My mom was in the birthing room with me. She'd held my hand through it all. Once my baby exited my body, my mom made her way towards the doctor as he was cutting the umbilical cord. My mom looked upon my baby and sad, "hell she looks like them," and walked out of the room.

Alaisja Nalani Ne'cole Creary was born on October 10, 1998! My baby, my daughter, my child.

She was so beautiful and small. She didn't cry; she just looked at me. Her hair had this perfect spiraling pattern. Her hands, feet and toes were so small and lovely. She had these eyes that captivated me. As she looked upon me, I knew she loved me and I loved her. This is my baby.

As I sat there taking all of her in, the neonatal nurses came over to retrieve her. They had to take her away for testing. I was not comfortable with that as just a month or so prior a newborn baby girl had been kidnapped from that hospital by a woman dressed as a nurse.

I'd started to panic a little... well a lot. One of the staff nurses came to my bedside to reassure me. She showed me the mother/baby wrist/foot bands which was used to identify baby and mommy. The staff nurse saw that my nerves were still on end. At which time, she promised me that she would be with my baby through each step and she would be the one to return her to me. That gave me peace of mind.

Since the missing baby, the hospital had implemented a new procedure which allowed the baby to reside in the room with the mother instead of in the nursery. I liked that concept. My baby girl was with me. Her dad and his sister came to visit that day. Alaisja was in her bassinet sleeping. Perry greeted me and immediately made his way over to Alaisja. He gazed upon her with the tear swelling in his eyes and a sincere smile upon his face. He said, "Princess, she's beautiful but she looks like Spring." Spring is his sister. Spring rushed over and stood next to Perry. Spring was awe of my baby girl. This is the first time of many of which someone would say, "She is so light; she doesn't even look like you had her." I did not respond; not sure why, but I didn't. Spring then washes her hands and then picks up her niece all while asking me her name. I said, "Her name is Alaisja." Spring loved the name but had trouble pronouncing it of course. Her dad had trouble as well. It didn't help that Perry also spoke with a lisp. I said, "It is pronounced *A-lays-jah.*" They loved and repeated her name several times through their smiles. Oh, the joy!

Perry had to be work so the visit was beautiful yet we had to wrap it up. Just before leaving Perry kissed Alaisja's forehead and then turned to me. I didn't know what to think as our relationship had been tumultuous to say the least. However, something magnificient happened; Perry apologized to me for the ill-treatment and promised that he would change. I had no feeling... I was child. Not only that I was numb to apologies from people who had abused me. Apologies didn't matter; actions did and even then I was closed.

After two and half restful days, it was time for me to take my little bundle of joy home. The staff nurses charged to my room came to see me off with well wishes. They brought in a newborn car seat complimentary of the hospital. I'd dressed my baby girl in her plush pink outfit and ruffled socks along with her Winnie-the-Pooh binky, which threw her outfit off but it was so cute. The nurses taught me how to properly secure her into the car seat. They commended on how well I'd cleaned and dressed her. They were surprised to see that our bags were packed and ready to go. I was asked if I were going to continue breastfeeding. I was determined to breastfeed my baby as breastfed babies are the most intelligent, so I was taught. I was ready! I'm a mommy.

Mommy such a cute word. For me, the word Mommy was different from Mother/Momma. Mommy is a happy-go-lucky version of the Mother. Mother established strength and responsibilities. Momma took on the burdens and plight of the day-to-day. Whew, the many hats of a child-bearing woman; but I was still a child... a teenager with a baby. I was a Mommy. Nowhere close to being a Mother. Not even equipped as a woman. But I had a child; an infant.

My mother came to pick us up from the hospital and took us to my grandparents. We all lived with my grandparents. The drive home was silent with the exception of whatever was playing on the radio. As we entered the driveway, a feeling of nervousness overwhelmed me. What was I going to do with this baby? Well, I have help, love and support. That lasted for quite a while. Alaisja and I were home. We entered the house and were greeted by aunts, cousins, uncles, friends...FAMILY. I was a little there but so far away mentally.

The first thing my cousins did was grab the loaded car seat from my hands. They adored Alaisja and showered her with love, affection and attention. My goodness, it was great and scary all the same. I found my grandmother sitting at the dining table in the kitchen. I made my way to her and pulled up chair next to her. She smiled and asked, "How you feeling?" My response to her was a lite, "I'm okay." She smiled and took a sip of coffee. That was a solemnly great conversation. It was just what I needed to snap me into the reality that I'd created; life.

It was hours before the house calm and semi empty. My grandfather exited the house. My grandmother made her way to her room. My mother and step-father went their respective places. Alaisja and I were together in our room/nursery for two. I'd laid my baby in her bassinette and I sprawled myself across the well-made bed. I could tell that my grandmother or Aunt Pamela had made the bed as the sheets were tightly secured and the spreadsheet was pristine which provided a level of comfort that all of sudden made me like I was home.

The smell of the room was that of potpourri and baby powder. As my baby lay quietly in her bassinette, I decided that would get a little reading in. I had six weeks to recover and get accustomed to being a mommy. After that, I had to think about re-entering school with a baby. My hopes of becoming a Lawyer and attending the University of Hawaii were so far away. But it was good to have had a dream. Well, I'd decided to read *A Midsummer Nights's Dream by William Shakespeare.* Somewhere between Act I. *The palace of Theseus* and the words *"…with duty and desire we follow you…"* I'd fallen asleep. Sweet rest it was.

As I woke from such a peaceful slumber, I looked over to notice that my baby was not in her bassinette. There were smells of southern style collard greens, homemade cornbread and sounds of everybody. I'd asked myself how long had I been asleep, jeesh. I made my way to my feet, and noticed a brand new pair of slippers were awaiting each foot. How pretty and convenient. I slid into my slippers and walked towards the sounds of the people in my home. My mother sat lively holding my baby girl. Mixing words with relatives and family alike about their feelings of me being a mom and how pretty the baby was. Typical!

I greeted my elders and smiled at my baby as I continued to the restroom to relieve myself and brush my teeth. Before I went into labor my Aunt Jocelyn had given me a sew-in so my hair simply needed to be brushed. I gave myself the once over and made my way back to the people. I didn't want to sit with the adults in the living room, which was considered rude and disrespectful. After all, children were not allowed to sit in the company of adults especially when they were talking. Children had a place and we'd better stay in it. But I was mommy.

....The Facts of Life

CHAPTER 8

Options or Choices

After the age of 19 years old, I decided to move out on my own; again. What an experience, to say the least! I moved into an apartment complex on Bert Road in Jacksonville, Florida. Let's just say the neighborhood was just a half a step above from my environment when living with Perry. I'd gotten myself set up rather nicely. I'd rented an upstairs one-bedroom apartment; it was cute and quaint just enough for myself and my little girl. I'd found a telemarketing position not far from the complex it paid well enough for the time. I was able to pay my bills and secure my rent payments on time; so to me that was good. Here comes that old dog sniffing around again… yep, my baby daddy needed a place to live. He'd gotten himself evicted. He came to me and said these exact words, "Hey, I need somewhere to go. I helped you when you was pregnant with nowhere to go." He was right… so I allowed him to move in, which re-kindled our relationship of horror. Oh gosh, whhhhyy did I allow him to do this? I would ask myself this question daily and never had an answer.

It didn't take long for the abuse to start. Perry worked nights and was often gone. The nights were quite peaceful but the days were too long. The weekends belong to me and my baby girl as Perry would hang out with his friends along with his cousin DJ. Perry cheated on me often with some wretched women and would bring back to my body curable sexually transmitted diseases. I would get treated and move on. I mean, what was I going to do? How do you leave your own home again? He was a good father to our daughter even though he despised me. I could take the foolishness as long as my daughter has her dad in her life; I would suffer through it. My life is no longer my own… my life…what life?

This nightmare lasted for almost 2 years. Soon after moving into my home; Perry's family followed suit. His mom and two aunts had both move into my apartment along with a cousin and great-cousin of his. Picture it… this is a one bedroom apartment on Bert Road in Jacksonville, Florida that now occupied nine (9) people. Lord, have mercy the apartment was just over 700sq ft. I'd started working at First Union National Bank in their Collections Department and I also took on a second job at the Family Dollar which sat adjacent to my apartment complex. I was the only person out of nine people that paid the bills. Yes, rent, lights, water and grocery. I was also starting to notice that I was becoming the sole caretaker for our daughter.

    The stressors of being a mom and sole provider were starting to take a toll on me mentally and physically. I can remember getting up in the mornings and simply rolling with the punches. Wake up, get the baby groomed, brush my teeth, comb my hair, grab one of my $7.00 dollar sundresses out of the closet and out the door we'd go. I would drop Alaisja off to KinderCare around the corner from my apartment. Take a walk through the good side of the area to take in the sunshine, smell the roses and admire the homes. One particular day, I'd stopped by the corner store to get me a bottle of water whilst on my way to work. As I was walking I'd allowed my mind to wonder about the what-ifs. What if I hadn't gone out that? What if I'd listened to my teachers? What I'd grown up with both of my parents? What if? That moment, I'd decided that I would stay with Perry to ensure Alaisja grew up in a two-parent household no matter what I had to endure. Life was no longer about my wants or my what if's.

    The days got longer and nights were much colder as I would lay solemnly in bed next to a man that didn't love, that didn't respect, that had blamed me for making him a father when he wasn't ready, a man that didn't see me. No, what was I supposed to do. Swallowing what little pride I had left, I let the abuse continue. But at least my baby girl was happy. I would suffer all of the sadness for her happiness. The tradeoff from mommy to Mother!

Life goes on and so do we. I'd received an eviction notice which gave me 7 days to pay my rent or to vacate the premises. I'd discussed this notice with the others that resided with me. Ironically, everyone had somewhere to go and they did just that. Left me hanging to figure out what I would do. A neighbor of mine with a small kid had asked me to babysit while she went to work that evening. My neighbor was a stripper at a local gentleman's club; Options. She told me that she would pay me $100.00 a night for sitting. I jumped on it because I sure as hell needed the money.

I'd looked after my neighbor's child for 5 nights. I was paid $500.00. I took that money to my rent office and explained to them that I would have the rest soon. I went to my neighbor and asked her how can work with her. She gave me the rundown. "You're going to have to go to the club at 6:30 pm and speak with the owner during the week. Do you have any clothes; like sexy lingerie? Why to want to this anyway? You don't even look like…"

"Listen, I'm about to be evicted. I just need to go for a night or two; you know just to make the money I need to pay my rent for this month."

I walked back over to my apartment and Perry's cousin was there. I told her the plan and she got really excited. "Girl, do it! You have the body and the face. Hell, if I could do it, I would." She and I went into my closet to find something to cute for me to wear for my one night only. Lo and behold, I was able to find this cute red bra and panty set that accentuated by ample bosom. Perry's cousin loaned me a pair of high heels that went perfect with my underwear set. After searching for something to wear; I made my way up to the gentleman's club for my interview. I walked myself up to the bar and asked for the owner and told her I wanted to apply to be a dancer. The young woman at the bar looked me over and chuckled as if she knew that I would be chewed up and spit the second the owner laid eyes on me.

Nevertheless, the young woman walked to the back of the club and entered a small office. Out walked this sultry seasoned Pilipino woman dressed in all black with the biggest jet black Peg Bundy hairdo draped in baubles around her neck and wrists. She made her way to young woman behind the bar and the slowly walked over to me and said, "What's your name, honey?" I replied, "Princess Booker." She then asked, "What's your real name, honey?" I'd stated, "That is my real name." The sultry woman smiled and said, "Be here tomorrow at 7. Not 7:01 but 7, honnneyy. Your bar fee is $10.00 and must be paid before you start. Write your name and number on this piece of paper." I smiled and said, "Thank you, thank you so very much. I'll see you at 7 tomorrow night." I walked out there as if I'd just made the best decision of my life. Not knowing that I'd just signed a lease to enter Pandora's Box.

I went home and Perry's cousin was sitting in my living room watching *As the World Turns*. She lifted her eyes from the television screen and asked gleefully, "Girl, how did it go? Did you get in?" I was like, "Girl, yes. I start tomorrow night at 7 and I can't be late." Perry's cousin was like send Alaisja to your mom's house so that way you won't have to worry about a babysitter. I did just that. My mom was happy to look after my baby although she didn't know why nor did she ask. Thankfully, she didn't ask.

The next day, I went into my job at First Union National Bank and worked my usual shift, attempting to collect payments from bank customers with past due loans and/or overdraft accounts. My work there was short of lack luster as I wasn't a great bill collector being that I was a bit of a wall floor. You see the once hot blooded teenager was not drowned by the plight of teenage pregnancy and real-life bills. To top that, fighting to survive and physically fighting to keep myself from being totally damaged by Perry punches. What goes inside of your house should never be discussed outside; one of my childhood lessons. The clock neared 4:30 pm, which signaled the end of my shift.

I'd become anxiously nervous about my moonlighting activity awaiting me. It's quitting time...

I walked home after my shift playing over and over in my head how the night would be. I couldn't really create an image as I'd never been into a gentleman's club. The only thing I had to hold in comparison would be snippets seen on t.v. shows and street movies. Anyhow, there was no turning back; I needed the money. I was looking forward to being able to pay my rent and possibly having a little left over to take my daughter out for ice cream and pictures.

I'd made it home and Perry's cousin followed suit shortly after. She looked at me and must've known I was nervous. She made a failed attempt to reassure me by comparing me to their cousin's baby momma who was successfully making a living as a stripper in Miami. I'd packed my outfit and shoes into a lil' grocery bag. Perry's cousin chuckled and said, "Girl, you can't use that. You need like a suitcase or something." I didn't have that. Perry's cousin went into my hall closet which is where she'd kept her things and emptied out a rolling suitcase. I must say, that suitcase was more fitting that a plastic grocery bag. I took a shower and brushed my hair, which was woven into a long sleek bobbed hairstyle.

I'd asked Perry's cousin to drop me off at the club so I get it popping. She cheerfully obliged. Once we pulled into the parking of the club, I was getting out the car when Perry's cousin jokingly shouted out, "Make that money; don't let the money make you!" I rolled my eyes and laughed... if you know, you know. There was a bouncer at the door who stopped me as I attempted to enter the building. "What you doing here?" I replied, "I came to work; it's my first day." The bouncer shook his head in disappointment, stepped aside and said, "You should do good." I didn't know what he meant so I just kept walking towards the bar where I found the sultry Pilipino woman waiting to greet all of the dancers. "You came huh honey? Where's your bar fee?" I forked over my ten dollars and was directed to the girl's dressing room. The night-shift was live and in effect. There was a DJ blaring all of the latest greatest. There were half naked women in exotic cloths and big hair. The entire area smelled of Cotton Candy body spray and shimmered with flakes of glitter.

My neighbor saw me as I entered the dressing room. She was so excited and I was so nervous. She asked me to her my outfit and I proudly did so. "Come on now, you can't wear that. I have something for you to wear." That lady pulled out the most risqué pieces of lingerie. It was three pieces; bustier, boy shorts and trained attachable robe... all red! I was taken aback initially but through the encouragement of the other girls, I put it on. Now here comes the magic question; "So, what's your stage name? Yeah, what's your stage?" I didn't have one. A fellow dancer exclaimed, "Hey, ain't yo' name Princess? Use that!" Hmmmmm never really thought about my name until that moment. Like seriously, I never really thought about the significance of my name; Princess. Ok, so my real name became my stage name... "PRINCESS."

Two of the dancers took me to the DJ booth to give me his mane for rotation. The DJ assured me that I wouldn't be added to the rotation until I had more days of experience under my belt. I didn't plan on being in there for days so I overlooked his confirmation. The girls advised me of the cost per lap dance and how to mingle and mix the room. It was quite demeaning yet alluring. The two girls left me to my own vices as they were missing money trying to show me the ropes. I walked through the loud dark club with nothing but strobe lights giving the allusion of red light special. As I strolled gingerly, a girl walked up past and whispered, "You're never going to make any money like that honey!" She was right but what am I supposed do, just walk up to a guy and asking him to tip me money? Yeah right. I was never good at asking for handouts. So, I found a seat at the bar. I wasn't old enough to drink legally so I literally just sat there gazing at the all of the goings on. Just so happens, I'd sat next to a seasoned retired guy named Bruno.

Bruno must've smelled my fear and could see how green I was to the lifestyle. He struck up a conversation with me by telling me how beautiful I was. He didn't say I was sexy; he called be beautiful. I nodded my head forward while giving him a pleasant word of "thank you." Bruno then asked my name. Here I am telling him my full government; "Princess Booker." He laughed and stuck out his hand, motioning for a handshake. I reciprocated and he said, "Nice to meet you. Now get up and let me see what you look like." I wanted to tell him to go to hell but that would defeat the purpose of me being there. I did as he asked and promptly sat back down. We chatted the night away on topics relating to our life experiences; mine were quite short while his 65 years of living were packed with colorful stories. Before I knew the DJ was on the mic, charismatically bringing the night to a close. I'd sat there talking to Bruno and had made absolutely NO MONEY! As I thanked Bruno for a lively conversation and made my way to my feet, he grabbed my hand and asked to see outside of the club. I respectfully declined and he smiled while palming $700.00 and said hope this is what you to keep you out of this place. It was more than enough. I thanked him and made my way to the dressing room to change back into my "regular" clothing.

After getting home, Perry's cousin was there again, sitting on the sofa waiting on me. "Sooooo, how did it go, girl?" "It went," I replied. "Did you make any money?" "Yeah, $700.00." "Girl, $700.00, what did you do? Show me how you were dancing!" "I didn't dance at all. I just sat there talking to this old guy named Bruno." "Well, they say conversation rules the nations." I went to shower off the residue of gentleman's club from my body and remembered the electricity disconnect notice that I'd received early that day. Oh damn, how could I forget about that? I guess, I better go back and try to make some more money. The honey trap!

The next night, Bruno wasn't there. That was the night I learned what a lap dance was. That was the night that made my soul cringe. But I needed the money! Suck it up Princess; it'll be over soon. My first lap dance was disgusting. This man beckoned me over to his table and gestured for me to get started. I stood there in my borrowed sexy lingerie. I started to sway my hips from left to right, remembering what I was taught by my good friend's mother… "Whine your hips girl." I did just that as the song played on and the man's hand made his way to my skin. I tried withstand the invasion to my personal space by convincing myself it would be over soon. The cost of a lap dance was $10.00 a song. He'd actually tipped me $50.00; I guess my whining skills had gotten better. That $50.00 didn't equate to the shameful guilt in my mind. But, I needed the money. That night I did about six more lap dances for $10.00 a song and received a little extra from guy. I would say, it was a good night especially since I was a novice… NOT!

Moonlighting as a stripper became quite overwhelming as my evening hours at the club started to take a toll on me. I was so tired in the mornings which didn't give much energy to arrive on-time and perform my best at my job with the bank. Needless to say, I was let go. Family Dollar didn't give me much trouble as my schedule was random and I could still work at the club. By now, I was being introduced by the DJ for stage performances. I'd acquired a new custom for my show. I'd gotten my feet wet and didn't even realize that I was about to drown. I'd gone from being one of two Black girls at Options to just one of the hustlers as more girls started to flock to the club due to the type of clientele Options attracted… money makers and spenders. Big tippers are hard to come by but are always appreciated.

These new Black dancers had started to saturate the club, which bombarded my income. I couldn't have that but I didn't want to work any other clubs as they many of them were in questionable parts of town and the clubs in the Beaches area were too close to home. I had my farm area locked in but it was costing me money. Now, what am I going to do? I need money! This girl name Tasha from Douglas, GA had an idea. She propositioned me with an opportunity for us to take a trip down to Miami. This was an opportunity for us to be guest dancers at a few clubs there. Now Miami, had all of the hot spots like the Rolex that attracted players, ballers, drug dealers, pro-ball players and riff-raff alike. I agreed to do this as you know; I needed the money!

CHAPTER 9

Where them dollars at…ching ching!

Tasha had it all planned out so I'd thought. We commenced to our road trip from Jacksonville to Miami. My mother still had my daughter in her care as at this moment in time, I wasn't fit to care for her nor could I give her a stabled home environment. I was on the go; the hustle was real and so were my bills. Get money; spend money! Such a broke mindset, but hey financial literacy was not yet a thought or understanding. Anyway, Tasha and I made finally made it to Miami after getting lost and ending up in some hick town in Alabama. Don't ask me how we ended up in Alabama on our way to Miami. Just know GPS wasn't a publicized software for the masses at that time.

Tasha and I had gotten lost and we were hungry as two American hostages in a foreign country needing food and water. As drove looking for the exit needed to get us back underway, we ran into a nightclub with a parking lot full of US and a bar-b-que stand. Tasha was scared to get out of the car; I wasn't. I'd walked over to the line of people waiting to place an order. When it was finally my turn, Tasha got out of the car and walked over to me. On the other side of the table was this burly Black man with his belly hanging over his pants, shiny gold teeth ready to take our order. I'd asked for the rib plate that came with two sides and a soda; baked beans, potato salad and a grape soda. Tasha leaned in and said, "Make it two of those, please." The burly man grunted and said, "That'll be $10.50." I forked over the cash and received our food. Tasha and I made our way back to her car to eat our food when we were approached by these guys whose southern accents were much thicker than mine and Tasha's. These guys were handsome; I mean each of there were so darn fine. We chatted with them as we ate our food. They gave us directions back to the appropriate highway. We said good-bye and nice to meet you and went on about our business.

We finally made it to Miami. We drove around for most of the morning in search of the club we were expecting to work at. We found it and decided that we needed to find us a hotel room for the night. We did that; El Palacio! It was gorgeous and gave us the hype we needed to build our confidence for work that evening. We checked in and made way to our room; it was exquisite. We relaxed for a while to catch our breath; let's get it started! Okay, so what are we going to wear up there? We decided on these bodycon dresses that hit every curve we had. We just knew that we had it going on until we got to the Rolex and saw these women with bodies of Greek Goddess. I swear every woman had a tight round ass that reminisced the shape of a Freestone Peach and voluptuous bosoms. Whew, I mean Tasha was quite smaller than I was and she had no booty nor did breast outgrow an A-cup. We were cute though, that should work in our favor.

Tasha and I approached the doors to The Rolex and was greeted by a bouncer with the biggest, broadest chest ever and a mouth full of gold teeth with diamonds sparkling through his grin. We told that we wanted to dance and he looked us over and chuckled. Bouncer gestured for us to follow him towards the manager's office. No turning back now! Tasha went into the office first. I think this is the first time I prayed to ask God to protect us. The office was full of men. Tasha came out adjusting her blouse and said, "It's your turn." Now here I am nervous as hell; but I went in anyway.

There was this guy sitting behind a desk. "Blyke, show me what you got." "Do you want me to dance?" "No, get naked." Oh gosh, naked; was he serious. I had to get naked in a room full of men and hope that they wouldn't take advantage of me. I prayed mentally asking God to let me make it out of this office unscathed as I undressed. The guy behind the desk gestured for another guy to come over and check me out. They forensically checked my body for stabbed wounds, healed bullet holes and stretch marks. He'd found the bullet wound on the outside bottom area of my right leg. He pointed as if to show the guy behind the desk what he'd discover. The man behind the desk asked me what happened. I told him that my baby daddy shot me. Every man in the room laughed with one saying, "Damn, she must got that fye!" Talking about humiliating. The guy behind the desk noticed I was embarrassed and not for being shot but for standing there naked. He asked me, "If you're shy in here how are you going to work out there?" I was silent. The man behind the desk gave his approval and then told me to get dressed. He told me that the bar fee would be $200.00 upfront. I said ok and paid him. I walked out of the office with all of my ego left in that room. I walked over to Tasha who asked, "Did you have to get naked?" "Yeah!" Tasha then asked, "Did you have to pay $200.00?" "Yeah." Well, I didn't have it so he told me that I could pay him before the night is over with," Tasha said. All I could do was nod my head and make my way to the dressing room.

That dressing room was full of exotically beautiful women; Haitian, Jamaican, Bahamian, Cuban and Black... there's a difference. The room had stations set-up for each girl to have access to their own mirror to touch up hair and make-up. Everyone minded their own business which worked fine for me. I wasn't much of a talker. Tables are turning fast! The hustle was real in Miami; you either get down or be clowned and I was too far away from home to come up empty handed. Get to work, Princess... you know you need this money!

Tasha did so good that night. She even met Trick Daddy and his entourage; that girl found her niche in the hustle. Me, on the other hand tried to find a way out of that place. I didn't have a car and didn't rightly know anyone that I felt comfortable calling to pick me. This sucked big time... But I needed the money! I started to work the floor sashaying around in my lingerie which was my gimmick. The guys liked it to say the least. I was approached by several men for sex; in that I would decline by saying, "I don't trick. I dance!" Some guys were insulted while others found it interesting. Getting to the point, I made my $200.00 back plus an extra $1K. Now, that was a good night! NOT! In Miami, $1200 was a slap in the face especially for the '99 and 2000.

Tasha and I woke up the next morning ready for the day. We'd decided to eat breakfast the hotel by the pool when all of sudden a news bulletin interrupted the regular broadcasted program announcing that R&B star Aaliyah had died in a plane crash. A moment of silence overcame the atmosphere to take in what we'd all just heard. How sad… but Tasha reminded me that we had to keep our mind on our grind. Let's take a ride and check out what the streets of Miami had to offer. We rode around to our hearts content. We talked about our children as Tasha had a one year old son and Alaisja was now two years old. Time truly flies right on by you especially when you're gone with the wind; just caught up in world of nonsense and sin.

We'd finally made our way to a side of town with a sign that read *The Pork and Bean Projects*… literally. We laughed as we didn't know the danger that we just subjected ourselves to. My girl and I were feeling a bit flirtatious and decided to let our hair down per se. I just smiled a lot and got a number or two. Tasha met a guy and started an instant relationship; that was her nature though… fast and loose.

Tasha had gotten so comfortable with the guy she'd let him in the car as he needed a ride to the neighborhood corner store. Tasha pulled off with this guy sitting in the back of the car as he gave her directions to the store. He told us that he was a rapper and that he had a new song out while handing the CD over the seat. I grabbed the disc and read it the title out loud, "Peanut Butter and Jelly?" He was like, "yeah that's that heat right there. Put it in man." I handed the disc over to Tasha and she put into the car's CD Player… and Boom! *"It's Peanut Butter Jelly time, Peanut Butter Jelly time…"* I must say it was catchy dancey in a Miami Bass kind of way. If you're from Florida or familiar with the sounds of Miami, then you know what I mean. As we were driving and dancing all of sudden, the guy pulls out a gun and robbed us. He stuck us up for all that we had; so he thought and told us to enjoy the music. Bastard!!!

That Negro robbed us!! Tasha was hurt and crushed at the same darn time. We drove back to the hotel. As we entered the lobby the lady at the counter stop us and asked us to approach the counter. As we got close, she told us that had balance to pay in order to keep our room for another night. I inquired of the balance and when she told us, Tasha told her that we couldn't afford as we had just been robbed. We told the lady the whole story in which she felt sympathetic to our plight and discounted the room. I pulled money from my bra and counted out the amount due. Tasha was so shocked so much so that she exclaimed, "Bitch, you had more money?" I said, "Yeah, I never keep all of my money in spot." "Do you have enough for us to cover our bar fee?" I replied, No!" I did but I wasn't about to pay $200.00 for her. The lady at the counter suggested that we try out a less sophisticated club, Take One over on NE 79th Street. We took her advice and did so.

Our first night at Take One was actually kind of funky in every sense of the word. Whatever popped up in your mind while reading, take it for what it is. It was not only it was also quaint and gloomy. You could smell the age of the carpet and the disregarded scent of exposed women. The dressing room gave bottom of the barrel... but hey I needed the money. That night Tasha looked up and met a guy that played ball for the Miami Heat. I met this lady with a body to die for wretched with AIDS. Yep, Sexy Black had AIDS and she made it known. I was glad that she shared some of her story with me as it scared me enough to stick to my rule, NO TRICKING!

What is tricking? I figured I would explain this as I've mentioned this a few times now. Tricking means to engage in sexual acts for hire. In short, slang for prostitution. Due to my previously history, I was afraid of sex. The word itself actually disgusted me. How unhealthy is that for a young woman at the start of her life to loathe intercourse. Where's the nearest therapy sofa?

Tasha walked over to me as I stood in the far right corner of the club gazing; she introduced me to the tall lanky fellow. His polished charmed glimmered amidst the cesspool. I welcomed his hello for some reason I thought he wouldn't be like the other guys; boy was I wrong. I learned at that moment I horny man is a horny man no matter his social economic status nor his title. The ball player invited us over to his condo for drinks and socialization. Tasha was uber excited, how could I say no?

We made it to the guy's South Beach condo in Tasha's car. We followed the instructions the guy had written down on a napkin. As we entered the lobby, the looks we got would make a person kill over. Nevertheless, it didn't bother us. Once we were off the elevator, we entered the foyer of this guy's place. Everything was immaculate; white & stainless steel. Loud music pumping. Wall to floor men and women. Cocaine lines and champagne. The smell of marijuana and liquor… It was definitely a party and I was out of my element for sure. But hey… ahhh I bet you thought I was gonna say….Nope. I wasn't about to leave my girl behind and I had to watch her back as she started to partake in sharing lines of coke with the masses. I had to stay sober. No way was I gonna be one of **those girls** and neither was my friend.

This older white guy; hold up wait, why am I always attracting old men? Anyway, this older white guy dressed in a black and white leisure suit approached with a glass of champagne. I entertained him pretending to sip and mingle. He complimented my skin and mentioned how much he adored "the chocolate sistahs." Blah blah blah, right? I finally made a b-line to the restroom while passing an occupied room and saw my girl Tasha with two other women and the ball player getting it on. Face down, feet to the ceiling and balls to the wall; they were going at it. I couldn't believe it. It was going down all up in that condo. There were only a few us not engaged in activities so we just all huddled up and talked. Before, I knew it the sun was coming and Tasha was approaching from the hall. "Girl, do you see my keys?" I replied, I have them right here. Are you ready to go?" She slowly nodded her head forward. I waved good-bye to my new comrades, two of which I am still in contact with 22 years later.

Once we were in Tasha's car I didn't ask any questions. She started talking about how much fun she had and how much money she made. She paused and said, "But I didn't have sex with him or nothing." I looked at her knowing full well she was lying. I mean, I'd seen their orgy with my own two eyes. Who am I judge… do you Boo! I didn't say that but I was definitely thinking it. Let that girl tell whatever lie she needed to, which would help her sleep better. For what is worth, she made $2500.00 that night. I only made $350.00 and that was my tips earned at the club.

We returned to El Palacio and the desk clerk asked us how everything went. We told her great and that we were going to check around as we needed a less expensive hotel and something closer to Take One. Now honey, less expensive meant cheap without it being a roach motel. We ended up at the Bay's Inn. You read it correctly, the BAY'S INN! We checked ourselves into the Bay's Inn and were given keys to a room on the 5th. The lobby attendant made sure that we understood the fifth floor not the fourth floor. We thought his insistence was a bit unwarranted we slowly learned why it wasn't. This room was nothing like the one at El Palacio. It was just a room with odd view of the city. Tasha and I started to map out our day. We counted our money and came up with a goal to meet which would have made this trip worthwhile. A knock at the door startled the hell out of us.

We glanced at each as the knocking paused and started again. Tasha shouted, "Who is it?" The voice from the other ended stated, "It's Joe."

"Girl, do you open that damn door."

"Why not?

"Dammit Tasha, don't open the door."

She did; she opened the damn door. There stood this big buff black shinny dude with a rack of dresses.

"Hi, my name is Joe. I saw you beautiful ladies checking in and wanted to see if you all were interested in perusing some of my fine designs."

I immediately said No and Thank you in one breath.

Here goes Tasha fast ass; my girl was on a paper chase and I was moving to cautious for the life. Tasha let Joe into our room with them dresses. I can't lie those dresses were lit for real. Tasha tried on a few and she rocked 'em all. She even found a cute lil' red one for me. Joe egged me to try the dress on. Curiosity won me over and there I stood with my sex appeal in this fine red dress. I loved it. The very next moment after Joe saw me in that dress, he says… "ya'll can have those for free." I was like no way. My momma once told me that if a man offers to give you something for free don't take it unless you know what's tied to it. I went into the bathroom and I took that dress off immediately. When came out of the bathroom, Tasha and Joe were gone.

I panicked and couldn't breathe; where's my inhaler, I couldn't find it. I took several deep breaths to allow myself the ability to calm down. I'd found my inhaler remember I had asthma. I found the room key and room out the door making my way to the elevator. Once I was inside a lady said to me, "You looking for yo' friend?" I replied, "Yes ma'am." She then said, "She's with Killer Joe on the 4th floor honey." In my mind, all I could think of is *what the hell is a Killer Joe and where in the heck is my friend. Why was my friend with a man name Killer Joe? Why is his name **Killer** Joe?* Jesus Christ! What is going on? I got off the elevator at its arrival to the 4th floor. Boy, I was hit with some much at one time.

I walked slowly down the hall. Some of the room doors were open and others were closed. Tasha saw me and ran to me with the biggest smile on her face. I didn't know what to think or how to react. "Princess, girl, Killer Joe is going to look out for us." Us? Who in the hell was us? Joe walked up slowly behind her and began to explain his operations to me. He told me that he owned the 4th floor of that hotel which is where he kept his whores. It was so many of them. He told me that he could offer us protection while we worked in Miami and ensure of safety as well as any fees associated with our hustle. I was shook but I knew I couldn't show or else I'd been eaten alive.

Killer Joe could tell that I wasn't picking up with he was putting down. He put his massively strong arm around Tasha's small shoulders and said to me, "I may have something a little different for you. Something that might better suit you than this right here." Don't' be shy you're welcome here on the 4th floor. I followed the two of the slowly, Tasha broke away and entered a room with occupied by three ladies who indulging; they were snorting coke. That was her thing I'd come to learn. Joe walked me into this room and introduced me to his "Bottom Bitch."

What is a *Bottom Bitch* you ask? I asked too and was hit hard with a reality that I was not equipped nor ready for. A bottom bitch is usually the prostitute who has been with the pimp the longest and consistently makes the most money. Being the bottom bitch gives the prostitute status and power over the other women working for her pimp; however, the bottom bitch also bears many responsibilities.

Killer Joe had left the two us alone in the room while he went to do what a Killer Joe does. This lady was so beautiful to me. I could see her beauty through the pain, tension and exhaustion on face. Her skin was still tight but her eyes looked as she'd been crying for years. Maybe it was the side effect of the drugs or maybe she had been crying for years. Perhaps it was a combination of it all. That beautiful woman looked me in my face and asked me what I was doing there. I explained to her the beginning of it all. How I got pregnant, became a single mom with no education, being broke and ending up in Options. She said, "Damn baby girl, that's a lot. But how did you end up here? Why aren't home?" I really didn't have an answer for that. There was a thick silence.

"Well, I'm from Atlanta, Georgia. You ever been to Atlanta? You probably haven't." She was right, I had never been to Atlanta. Hell, the first and only time I'd been to Miami was in 1986 on a family trip to meet my mom's then boyfriend's family.

"I came here just like to you did, to dance in these clubs and make some money. Until I met Joe. How old are you?"

"I'm 21 years old."

"Baby, why are you here? I have son 'round your age. I have six kids actually. I have seen my kids in 6 years. That's how long I've been here."

"Well, why don't you just go home? I know they miss you."

"I can't baby and if you and your friend hang around here much longer ya'll won't be able to leave either. His name ain't Killer Joe for nothing. Talk to your friend and ya'll get out here. Go home, baby. If she don't want to leave; leave her. Go home!"

Joe walked back into just as he'd left, soft and easy. "Hey there, Pretty Black. What you say your name is again?" I replied, "Keisha."

"I coulda sworn Tasha told me your name was Precious or something like that."

"No, that's just my stage name."

"Precious and Pretty Black, let me get ya'll some food and go over this my proposal with you."

"Listen, I don't do drugs. I do not drink and I'm nobody's trick."

Killer Joe laughed in admiration of my confidence. "Nawl, nie I have something else to talk to you about. It's all good." He said, standing boldly in front me gingerly rubbing his hands together.

The beautiful lady in the room quietly said, "Come on Joe, not her. She ain't no good for this."

Joe replied, "You like money, don't you baby? Hell, we all need it."

I sure as heck needed some money and more money than I was able to make in them strip clubs. I gave Joe a minute to give me the rundown.

That minute of time really blew me away but I was down for it. My end of the operation was completely legal. All I had to do was obtain AIDS prescriptions and sell them to Joe for $150 a bottle. Joe would then sell them to American doctors who would transport them to Africa and Haiti to treat those patients who could no access the necessary medication. Joe educated me on the types of prescriptions to look for. I caught on quickly. If Tasha didn't want to go back to the strip club that night, I was cool with it because I'd found my lane.

CHAPTER 10

Action

Tasha and I made ourselves ready for the evening. As I was getting dressed, Tasha threw over that stunning red dress I'd tried on earlier. I told her I wasn't wearing it because I wasn't able to pay the cost for it. Tasha told me not to worry about she had already paid for me. I paused, sickened by her statement. Nevertheless, the moment passed and I put the dress on baby. I was fine as hell… literally and figuratively. Tasha reminded me our goal as we made our way to her car.

We arrived to the club but something was a little off. I couldn't quite put my finger on it but something wasn't right. Even though I'd changed into one my costumes, I didn't work much as I watched Tasha all night. She was a real hustler in the club but this night was different. She was high and her actions didn't leave anything desired for. I was worried and angry; I felt like we should have left. Tasha insisted on staying. The mantra is, "we come together; we leave together." I stuck by the code. She didn't. The club closed and there was no Tasha. Everyone was leaving and there was no Tasha. I walked out to the parking lot. Her car was there but she wasn't. I stuck around for a bit but I couldn't wait any longer.

I started walking down the street in the direction of the Bay's Inn. Feet hurting due to the stripper heels that weren't made for walking on pavement. My heart was pounding because I was walking down Biscayne at 2:30 am. Ok, I was terrified. This car pulled up next to me and I just knew I was about to die. This girl leaned her head out of the window and said, "My cousin says he'll take you home." I reluctantly turned her down. Then she said, "Girl, do you know where you're at?" I didn't know but I knew I was safe. Anyway, I did recognize the girl from the club. I'd seen her a few times and she seemed friendly enough. I mean, it was just a ride. The hotel wasn't that far away. With apprehension and hesitation, I took the ride or should I say I took the bait.

Once I got into the car, I felt like I'd made a dumb move. So, here I go again praying that God keeps me safe. "Please God don't let them kill me." We got to the stop light and the girl jumped out of car. The guy sped off through the red light. I'd been kidnapped… Taken!

The driver of the car was this with long dreadlocks. Sitting in the back seat of the vehicle, I couldn't see his face. I remained silent as this was my only combat against the fear inside of me. I remembered something my cousin Fat Boy had told to me, "If you ever find yourself in a situation cuz don't panic. Panicking will get you killed." He'd told me that when I was maybe 16 years old. But I remembered… don't panic or you will be killed. I didn't want to die. Suddenly, I thought about the only thing in life that I live for; my baby girl, Alaisja.

We got to the Holiday Inn. Just before we exited the vehicle the guy said to me, "When we get out of the car don't make a sound, don't move until I tell you too. If you do…" That's when he showed me the gun. "Don't panic or you will get killed…" I didn't want to die, so I took my nw deceased cousin's advice. Maybe he was with me somehow. It was like I could feel his presence. That gave me solace in a condemn place.

The guy told me to get out of the car. I did as he asked. We walked into the Holiday Inn together and I waited as he checked in. We walked towards the elevators and he looked at me. I finally saw his eyes. My soul sank. "Lord God, please don't let me hurt me. If I have to go through this, please don't let him kill me. God, if he rapes me, please protect me like you did that night when Warren molested me. Let me not feel it. Please let my body go numb and if I survive, please let me forget." Another silent prayer. This was the first time I'd had a vivid memory of the first time I'd been molested. Isn't it ironic?

We were now inside of the room, just me and this stranger. This man who had taken me. My kidnapper. He put his gun on the bed and told me go take a shower. I did as I was told. While in the shower I wept in preparation for what was to come. I kept the sounds of my tears silent. I was so scared. I told myself to get it together. It'll be over and that maybe he would just rape me and then let me go. There was a knock on the bathroom door. It was him, "Ok, get out now." He'd said in this heavy Caribbean accent. "Oh Lord, Imma die." This man is from the islands, they all crazy over there.

Turned off the shower, grabbed a towel to cover myself with. I reached for my clothes but they were not there. He'd taken my clothes. "Don't panic, or you will be killed. Show no fear, Princess." I walked out of the bathroom covered only by a bath towel. I was dry enough to sit slightly at the edge of the bed. "You can relax. I won't touch you unless you want me to." Huh? I was confused. He handed me the remote control and told me that I could watch what I wanted to. I found an episode of *The Golden Girls* and watched. "Do you know why I took you?" I shook my head negatively. "I took you because you didn't know what you were doing? I saw you in the club and I watched you. You didn't belong there. You didn't know what you were doing." At the time, I didn't know what he meant but I've lived a little longer I realized he was right. I didn't know what I was doing to myself, my child, my life.

The room was silent again with the exception of the antics of those four zany women blaring from the television. I'd fallen asleep. When I woke up, the guy was sitting in a chair staring at me. I rose slowly from my slumber and realized that he'd been through my purse. "Princess Sharmara…" He spoke my name. "What a beautiful name for such a pretty gal. Tell me about yourself, Princess." I didn't know what the heck to say. I just sat there staring at him staring at me. He started to talk, telling me all about his childhood and what life was like for him as a boy growing up in the Bahamas. I was intrigued. He stopped when he realized that was engaged and asked me if I were hungry. I wanted to lie and say no but my stomach wouldn't let me. "I'll go and get you food. You stay here and do not leave this room." I assured him that I would stay put.

The guy left the room with me in it. There I was alone in a room watching Matlock and interested in the open safe where in which the guy had left a large stack of cash. Many thoughts ran through my mind. For instance, I can take that money and make a run for it. That might work if I knew where I was. I can just leave and run down to the front desk and tell them to call the cops. Or I could call the front desk from the room and tell them that I've been taken. Well, what of he had a set-up similar to Killer Joe. I could get myself killed. "Don't panic, stay calm and watch Matlock."

The guy returned with two bags of food. The aroma was tantalizing. I was so freaking hungry. He removed the plates of food from the plastic bags while asking me, "You ever had ackee and salt fish?" I'd never heard of such a dish let alone had I ever eaten it. I shook my negatively. He laughed at me. I thought that was odd. But okay, I need food. He'd sent the food before me as if dressing a dinner table. "Now, taste." I tasted the food. "You like, huh?" I like; I like it a lot. As I scarfed down my newfound favorite breakfast; ackee and salt fish, the guy continued where he'd left of in his story. But not before mentioning that I held the countenance of his mother and sisters whom he held in very high regard. I was shocked and thought to myself, *sooo you would kidnap your mother and sisters? Or how would you feel if someone had kidnapped your mother and sisters.* It was like he could read my mind or something but he said to me, "If someone even thinks about to touching my Modder or sistas I will kill them man, ya know." I nodded in agreeance and continued to eat my food and listened to his story.

He painted such a lovely picture of his island and the culture of his people. Somewhere inside me I wondered what my life would've been like had a grown up in the Bahamas as he did. It wasn't a bed of roses by far but the purity of their life seemed serene in sense. He spoke with passion as he described his boyhood and family relationships. He talked about God. He then the following shook me back into reality, "When I first saw you, I wanted to make you mine." All hell here we go; I'm being held captive. He says to me, "I cannot hurt you. It is something over you, you cannot see it but I can. This is why I cannot hurt you." This is insane God get me out of here.

"Princess Sharmara, I am glad you did not try to leave in my absence. I would have had to kill you." I didn't say a word nor did I look his way. I just kept watching the re-runs on television; *Touched by an Angel*. He told me to get dressed. I looked over the room in an attempt to find my clothes. He asked me what I was looking for. I told him that I was looking for my clothes. He says, "Oh, I threw those things away. Put on this dress I bought for you." I put it on and searched for my shoes. He says, "You have new shoes too." The dress was a flowing white sundress and the shoes were gold gladiator sandals. How soft; I loved it. Is that weird? He'd gotten rid of all of my things with the exception of my purse and its contents.

We were now leaving the Holiday Inn. I complied with the guy every step of the way. After leaving the Holiday Inn, we ended up at his condo on South Beach. It was in a much different location than that of the ball player Tasha had met. But it is nice just the same. Once we entered his condo, the guy asked me if I wanted some water. I said yes and he brought me a glass of room-temperature water. His place was decked out, very modern and quite chic. All white furniture and stainless steel appliances. His television hung high on the main wall in the living room. His spot overlooked the ocean and it was beautiful. I couldn't take it all in as I'd started to plan my escape.

I'd watched an episode of Oprah that was about women who were held captive in a man dungeon. I just knew this guy was going to put me in a dungeon and chop me up into little pieces when he was tired of me. I'd rather jump from the balcony and take my chances on whether I would live or die. While I was sitting there with these damning thoughts, the guy walked in to the living room where I say tightly. He wanted to show me the bedrooms but I wouldn't move. I could tell my decision had frustrated him but I didn't move. I couldn't move to be honest. He walked away and point to the left of him saying, "This is the restroom." He brought me a blanket and told me to get some rest because we had a busy day tomorrow.

The next morning, the guy woke me up. He gave me a new toothbrush and toothpaste kit along with a personal bottle of Listerine mouthwash. I was happy to have 'cause my breath was kicking like Karate. He hurried me to complete my basic grooming session as we had somewhere to be. We made it to the parking garage and I walked over to the car that I was familiar with. The guys bellowed, "Noooo gal, we are taking this car." It was a Phytonic Blue Metallic BMW. I liked it. He opened the passenger door for me and I took my seat just the same. We drove to the strip until he decided to park. We strolled the boutiques and I stopped in front of one store. I saw this dress in the window that caught my eye. I was caught up in the moment of window shopping and couldn't believe my eyes. Everything in there was so glamorous.

The guy said to me, "Let's go in gal. You like what you see here?" I was reluctant but I was like a kid going into a candy store. The guy grabbed my hand and ushered me into the boutique. I felt so out of place, but he didn't let my insecurity show. He beckon one of the female sales reps and advised her to give me attention. The thin sleekly dressed woman walked over to me, "Madam, come with me." I looked to the guy for approval which he gave to me and then I followed the woman. She took my measurements while admiring the fact that my breast were real.

The guy stood over at the check-out counter while the woman and I worked on my clothes. Another woman walked over to me with a glass of champagne and handed it to me. I looked to the guy for his approval, he raised his slightly towards my way and nodded his head in acceptance. Then, simultaneously, we took a sip. The woman cheerful doted on me as if I was the only customer in the boutique. I was captivated by this moment in time. I walked out of that boutique wearing a two piece cocaine white suit and a pair of designer heels that killed the game. The guy looked me over and smiled brightly at me. He held in hands more bags of clothing just for me. Before we went to lunch, he looked me over and found that he hated my hair. It was synthetic wig that I had fashioned into a neat French roll. I guided myself back to the car and then drove to me a salon inside of USA Flea Market.

He entered first and then me; the women in the salon knew him and all greeted him with glee. I stood there in awe of this guy. *Maybe he wasn't so bad*, I thought to myself. The lead stylist walked over to me, gave me the once over while saying, "I will take care of her for you. Give me an hour and she'll be ready." He gave the stylist a wad of cash and she went to work on my head. When she was done, she spun the chair around giving me access to see myself in the mirror. I almost cried as I'd never seen myself so beautiful. I had a sew-in with 22inches of human hair layered with precision accentuating my high cheeks bones and feminine facial features. My hair now matched my clothes. When the guy returned he walked straight to me and gently grabbed my right hand, "Prinnnn-cesss," he said. My name never sounded so lovely. I stood up and we exited the salon just as we came.

I wore hair like that for years after this, escaping the guy. I changed my entire look to match the experience. Imagine me! That was one take away from the whole ordeal, new attitude. They say clothes don't make you; I'd beg to differ as those clothes sure as heck made me rethink my whole life.

"Let's eat," he said. "What do you want, Princess? Tell me, what do you want and I will get it for you." My ghetto self, "I want some chicken or some pasta." "Perfect, I will get that for you my Princess." I was now this guy, Princess. I wasn't my own anymore, I'd gathered. My momma's words came flooding back once again. The cost of receiving gifts from man; was I ready to pay up? No, I wasn't. But, hey, there I was his *Princess*.

The day turned in to evening as we frolicked the South Beach area and then some. His cellphone rang… "I am on my way," he said aggressively. His countenance changed after that call. I tell you; his whole person changed. I was now afraid. *Was that call about me? Was he about to take me somewhere and leave me? Has the time come for me to pay the piper?* Don't panic or you get killed.

We'd made our way to the some apartments between Miami and Hialeah. I don't know where we were to be honest. Before he exited the vehicle he gave me instructions. "Don't get out of this car. There's a loaded .45 in the glove compartment. There's a machete between the console and your seat. If I don't come back in 10 minutes, take the car and go away." All of that registered very clearly for me. While I knew how to shoot a gun, I didn't know how to drive a car. I didn't tell him that though. I watched him exit the driver side of the car and walk a short flight of stairs. It was silent for a while with the exception of the light engine running. I'd started to pray again, *"Dear merciful Father, if you let me make it out this I promise I will do better."* All of a sudden, I heard these loud masculine voices. The voices got louder as the guy got closer to the vehicle. Two men followed rapidly behind him, one guy yelling, "Fuck, you Florida niggas. A petty $10,000. Nigga that's chump change to niggas like us. We from Jersey nigga we get money." The guy never once looked back while he made his way back to the car. With the driver door open and the two men from New Jersey still talking trash while standing in front of the vehicle, they guy pulled out this sawed off shot gun and killed the both of them. Don't panic…

The sounds of the shotty blared like a sonic boom to my ears. I didn't flinch, I didn't move. I just stared out the window and prayed.

The guy closed the driver-side door and drove off as if he was just leaving a peaceful evening with friends. I was nervous for the end because he was driving slowly away from a murder scene with me, the car all dressed up. If I were to get stopped, no one would believe that I was this guy's captive. He looked over at me, I could feel him eyeballing me. I didn't panic, nor did I show my fear. I intentionally suppressed every feeling and every emotion. "Do you want some pancakes?" He asked. I replied, "Yes." We drove to this remote diner and had pancakes in silence.

The next day was a new day, I took a shower and he adorned me in the outfit of his choice. Another all-white linen short set. He picked out my sandals and oiled my skin. This man never made an attempt to sleep with me intimately. He'd told me that I would have to choose him. He made me over to his image; *his Princess!* We went downstairs to lobby and awaited the valet, the driver pulled up in a clean candy red Porsche. My goodness, where were we going? I didn't know but it wasn't like I'd actually had a say so in the matter. We drove to Overtown area of inner city Miami.

We pulled up to this outlandishly pink home. This home was flamingo pink for no sane reason at all. The property had mango trees and orange trees in the yard. Just before he got out of the car, I asked him if I could call my mom. He rested his back against his seat and said, "No." I pleaded with him telling him that I needed to check on my baby. He closed his door and asked me why I never told him that I had a baby. I apologized and assured him that I indeed have a child; a baby girl named Alaisja.

"How old is she?"

"She's two years old."

"Where's her Father?"

"He's around but he's not." I left my baby with my momma to come down here with my friend. We needed the money."

He gave me his cellphone to call my mom. He told me that I had to have the call wrapped up before he returned to the car. I promised him that I would.

I dialed the number to my grandmother's house; no answer. Darn it, *please God let someone answer the phone*. I dialed the number again, and my mother picked up. "Hello..." the sound of my mother's voice shamed me. "Hello, she said again. I said, "Ma, it's me." "PRINCESS! GIRL, WHERE IN THE HELL ARE YOU?" YO' ASS DONE LEFT ME WITH THIS BABY. YOU AIN'T CALLED, AIN'T BOUGHT ME NO CLOTHES FOR HER. WHERE IN THE HELL ARE YOU." "I know Momma, please listen please momma, I don't have much time. Momma, I've been kidnapped. "Princess, stop lying you always lying. Yo' ass ain't been no kidnapped." "Momma, I promise I'm not lying this time. I have been kidnapped. I gotta hurry up because the guy is on his way back to the car now. He told me I'd better be finished talking to you before he gets back." "What the hell are saying, put that nigga on the phone."

The guy entered the car and I was still on the phone. He looked at me and said, "Hang up." "I can't my momma wants to talk to you she doesn't believe me." The guy took the phone saying, "Hello..." My mother heard his accent and let out the most horrific holler. She gathered her composure and asked the man what was going on. "I took her and she's with me." "Please let my baby go. I love her and her daughter needs her." "I will send for her daughter. But had you loved her enough she wouldn't be here with me now."

His statement to my mother struck a major cord inside of, "...had you loved her enough she wouldn't be here with me now." I thought about every area of my life where I felt the lack of affection. The love was there but the affection of love was missing. At that moment, I silently prayed to God asked him to help me be a parent. "*Lord, please make me the mother that you have me to be for my daughter that you gave me. I don't know what to do. I just want her to be loved enough so that she doesn't end up like me."* That was a sincere cry out to God from my heart as I really didn't like myself much. I had no clue who I was, what I wanted to do; I had no direction; yet I'm mom. If I have no identity then how can I teach my daughter of hers? How could I teach her to be strong and confident when I'm weak? Just how?

I knew I had to get away from this guy; especially after hearing my mother's wailing. My mother's cry moved something within me; she actually cared. Why would I think that my momma didn't care for me? My mother was a very emotional woman. I found that out early on in my childhood. I was the one who comforted her when tears flowed from her heart. I was the one that took the brunt from the abuse from her anger and frustration. I was the one who sat up in the middle of the night while she went through withdrawal during her addiction. When I fell from the handlebars of my cousin's bike and chipped my tooth, she chastised me. When I reported my abuse as a child; she was ashamed. When those eight girls chased me to my house; my mother locked me out and told me to fight. She never consoled me as a child. She pushed and pulled me. She gave me commands and words that prepared me to face a brutal world. I can recall being in the hospital with a collapsed lung and she forced me to get well. She didn't let me be soft at all. Outside pretty fluffy dresses and curly que hairstyles, I was tough as nails. Well, all of that came in handy when I started to plan my escape from this guy.

It was time for a mask; a mask that needed to be worn in this situation. Who shall I become? As we pulled away from the pink house, the car was silent. He looked upon and finally saw my tear. "Why you crying, gal? I told your mother that I would send for your daughter. You shouldn't be without your pickney and your pickney shouldn't be without her mother." His voice sounded sorrowful which shocked me; but it was exactly the response I was seeking at that moment. "Stop you crying, gal. Just stop it! There's no need for you to cry. I take care of you, my *Princess*. I take care of you." His Princess with a countenance that reminded him of mother and the innocence of his sister; is now the Damsel in distress. The mask.

It was still early in day and we were just riding around from house to house. He would enter each location and I would wait in the car. We'd reach the fifth or the sixth house, it was time. *"Lord please let this work…please."* As he walked to the car, I faked an asthma attack. I vomited, heaved, coughed, and faked shivers. All of this produced beads of sweat. The guy looked upon in fear. "Princess, gal what is going on with you? Are you okay my dear? What is happening to you?" Through waited breaths I said; "I… can't…breathe…" "I have asthma."

"My Princess, what can I do?"

"Take me to Wal-greens, I need some warm water."

Instead of Wal-Greens he got out of the car and went back into the house. He eagerly returned with a red cup of warm water and gently handed it to me. I sipped the water as if it were a struggle for me to swallow. I even made my hands shake like I had essential tremor. I took several deep breaths to initiate the effects of the symptoms subsiding. I looked the guy and said, "Thank you so much. I was so scared. I haven't had an attack in a while. Maybe the stress of all is this was too much for me. I just want my baby."

The guy had a solemn look upon his face; he'd felt bad for me. Good! That is exactly what I wanted him to feel. He drove off from the house from which he'd gotten my water. We made a slight ways down the round where he pulled into a nearby park. He motioned for me to exit the car. I did as instructed. He then exited the vehicle and walked over to me. Pulling me close to him, I could feel the heat of his breath as his spoke to me, "My Princess, I am going to take care of you. I will love you and your daughter but only if you allow me to. I can give you all that you need and some of what you want. You have seen me and I see you. Be with me, Princess."

Really? You really want me to *be with you* fool after all of this crap? You really think that I would ever feel safe around you? Do you believe that I would let you around my child? Hell, I wasn't even sure if I fit enough to be around my own child. These are some of things that ran through my head during his protest of affection. I couldn't believe this guy. However, what he was offering was heck of a lot better that what had waiting for me at home. At least, prima facie his word seemed bona fide. I could take the chance of being captivated with the look of being secure. I had to get away from this guy.

My eyes met his gaze and said, "Okay, I will be with you. We can send for Alaisja; but how?" His face lite up as he repeated the pronunciation of my daughter's name. "I love her name. I love her already. Don't worry about how we will send for her. I do it all the time for my son. He travels to me from the Bahamas all the time. It's simple baby." Oh now, I'm his baby! Good! That is exactly what I wanted. I smiled and played into the moment. He wrapped his arm around my waist and whispered, "You'll never be free of me. You're mine, Princess." Ok, this is not good. Am I playing this part too well or does he through my ruse. Either way, it's too late to turn back now. I have to finish what I've started. I have to get to away from this guy!

We finished the song and dance and re-entered the vehicle. This man told me that he had a surprise for me. My nerves were on end trying to figure out if whether the surprise was good or bad. He turned on a tune that I so enjoyed by Buju Baton, *Love Me Brownin'*. If you've never this song, it is a must listen to. As the song played on, I allowed my mind to bask in ambiance of times before this trip to Miami. Walking freely by the ocean of Jacksonville Beach and playing the sand with my daughter. The smell of my mother. The sound of my granny's voice. The taste of my grandfather's cooking. I wanted to go home.

We'd made it back to his South Beach condo. While upstairs he pulled out the most beautiful ruffled and shear in the right place night on the town dress. "You will wear this tonight." I happily agreed as I couldn't wait to put that dress on my body. I put on my dress and walked up behind and grace my neck with the most lavish jewel. He swept my hair and turned me to him, "Oooo my dear, you must wear hair up tonight." I agreed. I mean the guy did have great taste. He matched my looked in all white suite that accented his cocoa butter skin. He was actually attractive. He didn't have capture a woman against her will. He could actually captivate a woman. He slightly grabbed my right wrist and lanced it with a gorgeous bracelet. We were ready to step out for the evening. And that we did.

We pulled up to this prodigious house; it was breathtaking. You could hear the sounds of laughter and Soca mixed with Calypso equivalent to the smells of Jerk and Curry. It was alluring. This time I didn't have to exit the vehicle on my own, as a gentleman he escorted me out of the vehicle. What is he trying to do? I am not falling for this or am I? Together, we entered the home and the people welcomed us as if they were awaiting this guy's arrival. I was shocked and slightly mesmerized at how the people praised him. Who is this guy? As we walked through the crowds of people, I could hear feminine vocals whispering, "O' she is so lucky. My goodness who is she?" I looked around to notice that they were whispering about me. I had never received such attention. It was strange but it felt very good. I relished in this. I almost forget the fact that I'd been kidnapped. I almost forgot about my plan. *Girl, keep your mask on. Don't get gone with the wind.*

The party went on for hours. I can't explain all that went on because I had to keep my mind on the main things; home and my baby. This is a dangerous guy. He's a murderer and a kidnapper. I could not allow myself to even think of actually enjoying myself. This wasn't real; but it could be. I'd stayed with Alaisja's father through all of the abuse and ill treatment. Why couldn't this be my life? I could grow to love him, right? He hasn't hurt me not once. He can take care of me and my baby. *Girl, snap out of it; you're a damn prisoner!"*

Chapter 11

Get Out

After the party, we returned to his home. I'd finally slept in the bed with this guy; he never touched me. He didn't even wrap his arms around me to cuddle. He just let me sleep.

By this point, I really wasn't shocked just thankful. Waking up the next morning was quite shocking, he met me in bed with breakfast. Fresh strawberries, blueberries, pineapples mangos with a glass of orange juice and a buttery toasted English muffin; breakfast. This guy greeted with a well morning and reminded me that I was a moon and a man is a sun. The sun is bright and always blazing. The sun represents strength and endurance. The moon is alluring and calm. A lunar cycle and menstrual cycle both take approximately 28 days. The moon offers a subtle commanding presence. I was taught this analogy by a guy I'd dated when I was fifteen years old and living in Maryland. I'd forgotten about it until that morning. It was a refreshing and much needed memory for a lost girl.

Believe it or not we spent the day in. He started talking to me again telling stories and informing me of his plans for me. I was taught that a man always has a plan for his life, career, woman and children. But, this is not right; I'm his captive. We made it to a place where I was able to insert, "… I just need to go by the hotel and check on my homegirl." I'd told him all about Killer Joe and his whores. "I also need to get my clothes and my asthma inhaler." He told me that I didn't need the clothes. I agreed with him but assured him that I would definitely need my prescribed inhaler. I can tell that he wasn't very keen on this idea but he didn't say no. This mask seemed to be working just as I needed. It seemed to be evolving as the fit got just bit more comfortable.

"So, where's this hotel, gal?"

"I'm not sure, but the name is Bay's Inn."

"What gal, geesh that place?

"Yeah, that was all we could afford after we got robbed and all."

"Robbed, Princess you have no business…"

"I know, I know but I needed the money."

"Get dressed and I will take you."

We drove to the Bays Inn and pulled into the front of the building. "You have ten minutes, don't make me come in to get you." Just as I'd started to agree to his stipulations, his cellphone rang. He motioned his finger to me giving me the instruction to hold on as he took his call. I waited as instructed. The call seemed to have taken his mind away from what was happening at the very moment; which totally worked in my favor. "Prinn-cess, I have to run right fast. You go get your things and you'd better here waiting for me when I get back. I want you outside not inside that place for too long, ya hear." I agreed and slowly exited the vehicle. It was my time to get out and not just out of the car.

The security guard recognized me and said briefly, "yo' friend ain't here no mo'." I walked past him to ensure the guy didn't see us talking. Once I entered the building, I ran to the front desk, "Ma'am, may I please use the phone. It's an emergency; I've been kidnapped and I need to call my mom." The lady paid me no mind as I repeated my request. Finally, being fed up with me, she told me to use the payphone. I didn't have any change; I had no money. Thinking quick on feet, I called my Aunt Pam collect. Thank God she accepted. "Princess, where in the hell are you and what is the shit yo' momma talking about you been kidnapped?" "Auntie, I have but listen I don't have a lot of time. I need you to listen just for a second. Dial this number…" I gave my aunt the number to Alaisja's grandma Cookie. Ms. Cookie answered the phone and I immediately went to explain to her what was going on. Her being from Miami and all, it didn't take much convincing of how much trouble I was in. Ms. Cookie, put us on hold and called her son Tonio who lived in Miami. Not only did

Tonio live in Miami, he has street ties in Miami. Blessed be the name of the good Lord.

Tonio entered the call via three-way, "Look here Princess where you at?" "I'm at the Bays Inn." "The Bays Inn? What in the hell are you doing there? Man aye, how long you think you got before he returns?" "Maybe like 30 minutes." "Ok, I'm finna send my people to get you. They gon' be in a red pick-up truck. They gon' take you straight to the bus station and you better take yo' ass straight home." "Ok, Tonio ok."

Ms. Cookie said a quick prayer for me and reassured me that I would make it through this. I was a bit skeptical; heck I was a lot skeptical. This had to work. I paced in the lobby constantly looking out the door. The security guard said to me, "Babygirl, I'll let you know when yo' people pull up." I heard him but I didn't. Just pacing the floor with my head bobbing up and down in panic, I slammed right into Buju Banton. Why did I have to meet him like this? I loved him as a fan and now I can't even get his autograph. I grabbed me by my shoulders and told me that he'd my phone call. His smile blessed and he told me, "Jah is with you black child." Just then, the security guard whistled, my chariot awaited. I ran as fast as could to the door. Just as I neared the red truck, I saw the guy pulling into the Bays Inn. "Thanks him!" These two guys were in the back of the pick-up truck. One jumped down from the truck and lifted my body like a piece of paper and handed me off to the other guy. They pushed my head down and grabbed their guns, I was out of there.

As long as I was in Miami, I felt like he was going to find me. The guys in the red truck did just as Tonio told me they would. They took me the bus station and gave me a few dollars to travel with advice to not speak to anyone. Once in the bus station, I used the payphone again to call my Aunt Pam who connected my mother via three-way call. The cost of the ticket was fifty dollars, which my cousin Louie had paid for. I went to the desk to pick up my ticket and waited for the call. The entire time, I kept watch of the entrance, making sure the guy didn't come to get me before I could catch my bus.

Bus to Jacksonville was called over the intercom. I jumped up so fast with ticket in hand. I was the first in line. I was still in Miami and in danger. I wasn't free until that bus left station and was on the road out of there. Once that happened, I was free. I had gotten away from that guy and was on my way home to my daughter. The entire ride I remained silent. I only prayed and talked to God. *Lord, thank you for answering my prayers. Thank you for keeping me alive. Thank you for letting me out!*

The bus pulled into the Jacksonville station. I looked out of the window expecting to see a familiar face but there was no one waiting for me. I figured surely my momma was awaiting my arrival. Maybe she's inside the station. I walked hurriedly to the inside of the building. There was so many people in there. I stood in spot looking for someone that was looking for me; there was no one. No one was there for me. I made my way to the nearest pay to call my mother. After the third ring, "Princess?" my mother asked. "Yes, ma'am. I'm here." "You're where?" "I'm here momma, I'm in Jacksonville. I just got off the bus." "Oh baby, how are you going to get home? I paused for a moment then realized that I had the money the guys from the red truck had given me. "I think I have enough money to catch a cab." "You got money? Why you ain't tell me you had money? Well, I'll see you when you get home." My heart sunk a little further than where was. I really thought someone would be there waiting for me. There was no one.

I walked just out the front doors of the bus station and found a small row of cabs. I walked to one of the vehicles and leaned slightly into the passenger side window, "Can you take me home, sir? I live in Atlantic Beach." The cabbie told me to hop in and I did. The cabbie drove me the 37 minutes from the bus station to the front of my grandmother's house. I paid the guy and exited the vehicle. I walked slowly to the door and knocked. After wrapping for a minute or two, my grandma opened the door. She said not a word, just stepped aside and granted me access. My momma came to the edge of the living room, looked me over and turned around and went back to her bed.

The room my grandparents had created for me and my baby was still there but with stuff everywhere. I went into the linen closet, grabbed a blanket and made my way to the sofa. I was tired and needed rest. The sun came up and it was time to rise; no laying around in that house. When the sun comes up, you get up. I could hear the pitter patter of my little ones feet; it was refreshing. I sat up to greet her but she didn't come to me. She went straight to the dining table. I walked over to her. I didn't know what to say. I just looked at her as she looked at me. Snapping out of it, I started breakfast. My mom entered the kitchen with a look of disdain and disappointment. "O' you gon' cook?" "Yes, ma'am, I can cook." "Well, that's the least you could do." "Yes ma'am." The silence was confirmed by her piercing looks. We sat down to eat breakfast.

The day went on and no one said one word to me about anything. I just went on about hearing faint whispers of everyone's opinion of me. My baby had aged and I wasn't there to see it. She was walking and talking and had made my granny's place her home. I felt like she didn't needed me. I didn't realize how long I'd actually been gone. Time can be an illusion, a real method of deception. You know that's how hypnosis takes place; by using suggested implications of time.

The next day home, I realized that I'd lost my apartment. Of course, I did. I didn't pay my rent. How could I? My grandmother sat at the dining table sipping a cup of coffee. I sat down next to her in an empty adjacent seat. "You alright." She asked. "Yes, ma'am." I replied. "You stay here, Princess, as long as you like."

"Yes ma'am."

"Have you eaten?"

"Yes ma'am."

I walked into my childhood bedroom. It was exactly the same, with the exception of my Uncle Sonny's clothes hanging in the closet. I walked around in a circle taking in all of the memories both good and horrifying. I sat on the bed and exhaled heavily. In walks Alaisja straight to me; she hugged me. How did she know I needed that? I felt her warm little hands on my neck as she embraced me. She looked as if she understood what I feeling inside. How could she know? I reached in for one more embrace and I squeezed her tight. She didn't push me away. I needed her. God knew that I needed her.

The days turned in to weeks, the phone rang; "Princess, the phone." Who would be calling me here? I made my way to the kitchen as the house phone was stationed there. My grandmother handed me the receiver, "It's some man." I thought it was Alaisja's father but it wasn't. It was the guy! "Prin-cesss, I only wanted to protect you. You can't see what I see, gal." My body froze. How did he find me? How did he get this number? He's gonna kill me, I know it. "I can hear you breathing Princess." The guy stated. "I know where you are. If you mention me or anything about me, I will know. And I will kill you." The phone call ended with the dial tone sounding off in my ear.

I've never talked about this until 4 years ago.

By the way, after being home for a month or so, I went by Options looking for my friend Tasha. She was really on my mind. I worried deeply for her. As I entered the club, it was totally different. The music was different, the atmosphere was different, the clientele was different; it was different. I was bombarded by a group of familiar girls.

"Where have you been, girl?"

"Hey, has anyone seen Tasha?"

"Yeah, she's in the back and she told us how you were down the getting off!"

"Getting off? What you mean?"

"Where's Tasha?"

As I made my to the back of the club heading to the dressing room, I see Tasha walking out all confident. My worry for her turned into angry. I wanted to snatch her whole face off. I approached her enraged and ready to throw down. Gemini, one of the dancers who knew me, grabbed me off my feet saying, "Princess let it go, she ain't worth it girl. What happened to you?" The bouncer saw the commotion and demanded that I leave the club. I did as he asked. That was the last time that I saw Tasha even though she still crossed my mind from time to time. I still pray for her and her son.

CHAPTER 12

Drugs, Sex and Mayhem

I've been home for quite some time now. I'd found a job at Subway working the night shift over in Arlington near Burt Rd. It was quite a ways from my granny's house but riding the city bus wasn't anything new for me. I didn't know how to drive so that was my main source of transportation. I had the transit scheduled down so I never arrived to work late. For nothing, I may have been early for each of my shifts. The job paid five dollars and seventy-five cents an hour. That was good pay as I didn't have rent to pay since I lived with my grandparents for free. My meals were free at the job so that helped too.

I'd arrived early for my shift and decided to sit in the lobby until it was time for me to start. Usually, I would go into the back and help with prep work. This day, I'd decided to sit and chill reading a novel by Diane McKinney-Whetstone titled *Blues Dancing*. The cover of the book reminded me of the movie, *Devil in the Blue Dress* starring Denzel Washington. Not quite sure why though. Enthralled by the descriptive narrative, I didn't hear my name being called until she tapped me on my shoulder. It was Lily Green, a girl I'd met during my stay at the Savannah Job Corp Center. I was very happy to see her. It was a welcomed surprised which lit up my day.

I'd admired Lily for her tenacity. While at Job Corp, Lily was a bright student if not the brightest. She had a voice reminiscent of Whitney Houston and CeCe Winans. That girl could sang! She was on every leadership committee at the facility. She was the go to person for any problems we experienced in our dorm area. So, seeing her brought me joy. I stood up to meet her friendly embrace as she introduced me to her fiancée and showed me her dazzling diamond ring. I was so very happy for her. I didn't expect anything less for her.

We sat and talked about our lives after Job Corp. She explained to that returning to her mother's home was simply too much pressure. Her mom was very religious and guided strictly through the Christian faith. Seems as though Lily had grown tired of living through her mother's eyes and needed to feel what life was like in her own walk. I didn't tell her about my trauma. I played into the narrative that life is good. You see by now, I'd figured out my masks were interchangeable. Let them speak and give them what they want to hear.

Lily and her fiancée had moved to the Jacksonville area due to his orders in the Navy. She was excited at the opportunity to become a Military wife. I applaud her for her choices and wish them well in their life together. He seemed to be a nice guy; don't they all. She and I exchanged numbers and went about our way. It was time for me to clock in to work and commence the shift change.

Lily and I talked for a while before I started we started meeting one another on my days off for lunch. I would stop by her house before going to work as she lived ten minutes from my job and have a cup of tea over lively conversation. Her fiancé was rarely home due to rigorous work schedule. So, it would be mainly us girls; which was welcomed. This went on for a few months before Lily asked me to become her roommate. The fiancé had received orders which took him out to sea. That would mean Lily would be alone in a city where she knew no one with the exception of myself. I told her that I didn't think it would be a good idea for me especially since I wasn't alone, I had a child.

Lily assured me that there would be room for the three of us. She also told me that had having a child in the house would bring her joy since she wasn't able to have a kid of her own. I sympathize with her. She was the only child of her mother and barren. I conceded and moved in with her. My mother was not happy with my decision for obvious for reasons. My grandmother left the door open for my return should I needed to.

Alaisja and I moved in with Lily. Everything started off on the right foot. I would pay two hundred dollars a month. I was responsible for the food consumed by me and Alaisja. That was fair. The apartment was spacious and very nicely decorated. The room we inhabited was more than enough. Lily and I got along great until she received the call that would devastate her life at the time. Her fiancé called and called off the wedding! Lily was distraught, anyone would be. She'd hung her hat with this guy.

Lily didn't work so the disengagement put her in a place with no income. I was only making minimum wage and the rent for that month hadn't been paid. The fiancé didn't pay the rent before he left. What a douchebag, right? He's sent his new girlfriend over to collect his things a few day after his gave Lily that horrible news. The heffa arrived with two of her friend girls and told Lily that she needed to get her man's stuff. Of course, Lily was not very receptive to this woman and neither was I. How dare she come to another woman's house really believing that she would be successful in her endeavors? "Get in blood, Bitch!"

That evening Lily and I packed his stuff and threw everything in the dumpster. He had the audacity to call Lily damning her to hell for getting rid of his things. Ninja please, get a life! He that Lily had no income and nothing saved. He knew the predicament that he was leaving in her in. Damn fool!

What the hell were we going to do? I couldn't go back to my grandma and leave my homegirl hanging. That would have been messed up. We could figure out way out this together, right? I could get a second job and help Lily gain employment. I brought this idea to the table during a conversation with Lily. That very moment is when I saw her first time; her mask was removed. "Princess, I can't get no job. What I look like working?" She'd looked like a person who need income to keep from being put out on the streets. Lily expressed to me how she above working a menial job. She could see her wearing a uniform and making sandwiches for people. Well damn, that's is exactly what I did for living. I'd never! How dare she? Well, she did; now what?

Lily had obviously had something else in mind; little did I know she was about to get it on and popping. I took Alaisja to my mother as I had to increase my hours at Subway to help more with the bills with Lily. My mom understood and I promised that I would visit on my days off and that I would be back to get Alaisja as soon as I got situated. Perry would stop by to get Alaisja often. Their father-daughter bond was strong. Perry was a good dad. He taught our baby girl so much. They would play, draw, dance and learn. Perry's an amazing artist. He's self –taught and naturally talented. That was passed down from his mother to him and now to our daughter. Alaisja had Perry wrapped around her little fingers. I loved that for her; truly I did.

After working a double shift at Subway and having to close the store on my own, I walked home that evening only to arrive bombarded by the scent of marijuana, loud music, a room full of ninjas and loose women. I was pissed off. What in the hell is this? You mean to tell this bitch couldn't get a job but had the nerve to through a party. I straightened my posture and decided not to pass judgment as this could be a rent party.

A rent party is a social gathering where in which a tenant struggling to pay their rental bill throws a shindig charging individual an entrance fee and additional charges for food, drinks etc. with hopes of coming up with enough money to cover cost of rent.

I'd figured if Lily was trying to raise money for rent, how dare I be mad. We needed the money. Our apartment was packed. I was exhausted from work and walking; I just wanted a shower and my bed. I had to shower in Lily's bathroom as my bathroom was now public access; it was disgusting. I locked myself in her bathroom with an apparatus pent up against the door to keep anyone from coming in on me. I finished my shower and made my way to my bedroom and locked myself in there as well. I'd pushed my dresser up behind the door to prevent any inquiring individuals from coming into my room.

I didn't get much sleep that night. I tried to block out all of the noise by blasting the radio station 95.1 WAPE. I can't remember what music was playing on my lil' radio but it didn't help to drown out, *Feeling on yo' booty...* "by R. Kelly blaring. Just loud for no reason! I was pissed off but remained calm as I'd convinced myself that this girl was throwing a rent party. I hope this was a damn rent party otherwise I didn't understand the need for this foolery.

I got the next morning to get my day started. As I excited my room, I noticed the radio was still on but low. The stench of party lingered in the apartment. Lily's room door was open which was odd for her. I peeked in on her and saw in bed with two men another woman. I couldn't eyes. I kept my composure, ensuring that I didn't wake them. I did not sign up for a brothel. I made my way down the hall to enter the living room; the place was a wreck to say the least. I glanced over towards the kitchen; how could adults be so filthy? Damn it; let's clean this shit up.

I turned on some smooth jazz by Cassandra Wilson. She's a favorite of mine. I'd stolen that CD from stepfather; he didn't miss it. Cassandra's raspy voice bellowed in the background as I moved through every nuke and crevice cleaning to sanitize. Lily woke before her guests. She sashayed her small over to the kitchen's counter, propped her head supported by a folder onto the surface and said, "Girl, I was going to do all of this. You ain't gotta do this by yourself." What I wanted was an apology for her to tell that she had her portion of the rent money. That didn't happen though.

Lily's guests woke and made their way out of our apartment all unescorted. They casually left; no words no gestures. That was fine by me as they weren't my friends. I'd found out later that Lily didn't even know those people. She'd met a few guys on the chat line and invited those strangers into our home. Lily made friends with the woman that lived in the apartment which is where the additional women came from. I couldn't believe her. I mean, what the hell was she thinking? Did not know of the danger she'd put us in? She didn't care, not at all.

Later that day as I prepared for work, Lily and I had a brief conversation about the night before. I'd asked her about her portion of the rent. I didn't even mention how upset I was about the party, as that was second to the money. Lily told me that she would have some of the money by the time I got off from work and that she was working on the rest. I already knew how she was coming up with her half; she was tricking! Damn it, man, why? This girl was way too smart and beautiful to resort to such acts. What made her want to do this? I guess she needed the money.

I went in to work and while in the middle of my shift, in walks this chubby, black ball of attractiveness. He had a mouthful of gold teeth that shined bright in the dark. He moved very easy. I glanced out the window and noticed that he'd exited a candy-painted Suburban with clean 24 inch rims. My kind of guy from the looks of it. Accompanying him was his friend, who didn't impress me at all. His vibe was off-putting as he attempted to mack me with tired lines to express his interest in me. I stopped him from talking to me and told him that I wasn't interested in him.

I turned to my kind of guy and asked him name. He told me… his name was Kirk. "Hi Kirk, my name is Princess. What Kind of sandwich do you want?" He asked for a ham sandwich, but I gave him turkey. I explained to Kirk why turkey was better for him than pork. He was intrigued and our conversation moved forward as I made his sandwich the way I knew would like it. His friend lingered idly by as Kirk and I got to know one another over the making of a foot-long turkey sandwich from Subway. Kirk's friend patience had run out during our love connection. I wrapped the sandwich and handed it to Kirk. "This one's on me." The look on Kirk's face showed him to be blushing through his licorice colored skin. He was cute.

Kirk thanked me and turned to leave the restaurant. I stopped him, "Hey, what's your phone number?" Kirk asked, "You want my number?" "I sure do." He handed his friend the bagged sandwich and eased his way back to the check-out counter where I stood. "Gimme a pen?" I forked over the pen and watched him write his number down. "You're gonna call me right?" I responded, "I might." He chuckled and they left the store. I went about my shift watching the time closely as I couldn't wait to get off. It was slow that night and I'd left my book at home. I cleaned the bathrooms and mopped all of the floors. I worked on prep since I had the time. This would help out the morning shift as they were usually busy. My manager would find my actions favorable.

I closed the store and walked home that evening. I got to the door and heard loud music again. I smelled marijuana again and was smacked in the face with it as soon as I opened the door. Oh gosh, not again. I didn't even look in the living room, I just kept marching forward down the hallway, heading to my room. Guess who I bumped into in the hallway coming out of the bathroom. It was Kirk! I spoke to him as if I hadn't just met him earlier that evening. "You live here?" Kirk asked. With an attitude of disappointment, I replied. "Yeah, I live here." I was so taken aback at seeing him. He was that kind of guy, a chat-line bandit; how unattractive. I walked right on past him and went into my room.

As I prepped myself for my bath, there was knock at my room door. Aggravated and terribly pissed, I said, "Who is it?" It was Lily. I opened the door slightly ajar, just enough to see the small of her face and to hear her words. "What girl?" I asked.

"Kirk says he knows you."

"I just met him earlier at work. He doesn't know me."

"O, he asked me to come get you."

"I'm not going out there."

I shut my room door in her face. I wasn't going out there. I was not with that. What they had going was not my scene. I took my shower and went to bed, leaving them to their night. Man, was I disappointed. I liked Kirk.

The next morning, I woke to see Kirk leaving out. He saw me and double back, "Hey Princess, call me okay." I replied, "No, you slept with her. I am not calling you." One thing about me is that I do not sleep with my homegirls men or men they've dated. That is a violation from my personal code of ethics. I wish I might!

I made myself a cup of coffee. The house was remarkably clean. The smell of marijuana had diminished. The place actually smelled of bleach and lemon pine-sol. Kudos to Lily and her guests of the evening for their display of adultness. I found the television remote in the correct place, turned to the Lifetime station for a good ol' drama. I was off today and wanted to relax a bit before heading to my granny's to spend time with Alaisja and family. Life wasn't perfect but I was on my way to stability.

Lily found me in the living room and made small talk fixing herself a cup of coffee. She offered to top mine off and I accepted. Lily awkwardly sat down next me. "What this heffa want?" I thought to myself. She better not try to come on to me. I didn't know what to expect from her anymore. She'd shown me a side of her that I never anticipated. "So, you that guy Kirk?" Lily asked. "Yeah, what about him?" I stated. "He really likes you." "Girl, please. He can't like me if he slept with you." "Princess, we didn't sleep together." "He just stayed because it was late, but he talked about you all damn night. It was quite annoying if you ask me." She told that she slept naked and attempted to entice him but he rejected her. I was impressed and flattered admittedly. I decided to give Kirk a call.

After catching a few Lifetime dramas, I decided to get myself up and at 'em. I checked the bus schedule to ensure I made to the bus stop on-time to catch the next one heading towards the beach. I called

Kirk just before I walked out of the door to tell him what Lily had told to me. He answered. We'd talked longer than anticipated and I missed my bus. I told him that I had to go in order for me to be on-time to catch the next bus. I had to go see my daughter. Kirk offered to take me. I reluctantly declined but he insisted so I took him up on his offer. Kirk was at my door within the hour as promised. That was the beginning of a 20 year love affair. Kirk is the only man that I've ever loved and ever will love.

CHAPTER 13

Kirk had come into my life and swept me off of my feet. You see Kirk was a hotboy. You know the "I'm not always there when you call but always on-time" type of guy. The mystery of lured me in deep. He was fun and exciting. He was sweet and comforting. He was strong and masculine. He was smart yet open to learning. He was! He is! I was like a moth to a flame when came to Kirk. Being with him made me want for more. I had no way of knowing how to get to the more but I wanted it. Kirk and I a lot of time together. We went on dates that catered to my daughter.

Still living with Lily, things started to get tight. Her sexual escapades were starting to take a toll on our living situation. The girl had even started popping ecstasy pills and drinking heavy. She wasn't concerned with bills; she was just looking for her next good time. I couldn't live like that. I couldn't live with her anymore. It was time for me to get out! The money I was making at Subway afforded the opportunity of simply getting by. What can I do? Options was just down the street from where we lived. I could go and work there during the day and work the night shift at Subway. That's what I did. I didn't tell Kirk as I was too shame for that confession. I never even told him about being kidnapped. The first time he'd that story was seventeen years after meeting me.

Things were different for me now. I was dancing at Options and making decent tips. I'd put on that salacious sensual mask and turned up the sexy. I couldn't go by the stage of Princess anymore. I needed something more fitting, and Honey Love was born. I'd picked up a few moves during my time at Take One. Old habits die hard and if you're not careful new ones will form. The money was good for a while but in the industry you learn quick tips are not sure thing. I needed a hustle. Many of the dancers had serious or budding coke addiction. I figured that I would find a lane as a third-party supplier of the product.

I didn't bother helping Lily with the rent anymore. I packed my things and moved back into my granny's house. I was a little older and much more mature. Life has a way of doing that to a young person who decides to jump of the porch before time. I pulled one of my cousins to the side and asked him to front me my first batch of cocaine. He didn't take me seriously but my persistence wore him down. He became my link to the cocaine, the yellow not the white. I made my first move the following weekend. No one would have pegged me for the type as my image was more Marilyn Monroe meets Brandy Norwood… the sexy cute black girl next door. I didn't make much noise when I entered the building but my presence was definitely felt. A lady should always make an entrance.

I sold coke to the girls at the club under the guise of a stripper. I wasn't a good dancer so I would pay the DJ to skip name during the stage rotation performances. I did get on stage sometimes to keep up the façade of it all. Money was definitely being made. I was able to maintain my job at Subway for a time. I was even promoted to a management position which increased my income. My relationship with Kirk had gotten a little strained as I was not as available as I used to be. I'd started lying to him to keep my hustles a secret. He knew I was lying but he would still show up for me. He still does.

This went on for years me hustling and flowing. No one knew what I was doing with the exception of my cousin and my clients. I'd made some new homegirls and started clubbing hard. I was on the scene from Jazzco to T-Birds. From the Paradome to Late Night, I was there. By this time, I'd started drinking socially and smoking weed. I didn't smoke weed in public as I thought to be unladylike. The Purple Haze had me in a trance. The Hypnotic had me chokehold. Those things would become vices known as strongholds. I never popped a pill or did any other drugs, I was too afraid. I saw what addiction had done to my family. I saw what such habits had done to girls. I couldn't let that happen to me. God wasn't gonna let that happened to me.

Somewhere in between all this a relationship with God was being created. Even though my sins seemed to be developing into multitudes.

Before I knew it innocence was lost to struggle and painful reality. A few years had flown by. Alaisja was now I school; I was still enamored by my fantasies. Caught up in the rapture of going nowhere. But, it seemed to be working; I was still alive. Kirk's presence in my life had all but faded away. He would still stop through from time and I would attempt to hide my life from him. Alaisja and I had our place which I'd decorated with exotic plants, earth tone furniture and décor. My space screamed afros, incense and bright lights. Love beads, mood rings and candlelight. I had gotten into the Neo-Soul trend with huge dose of UGK. While I wasn't banging diamonds against wood, I sure knew how to roll a mean Backwood.

Alaisja had her own room which didn't resemble the ethic basis of the rest of the house. Her room for fit for princess; pink and purple with a slight hint of cream. She had whatever toy her heart desired with the exception of those Bratz dolls. I couldn't stand those things. Alaisja was full of love, sugar and spice and everything nice; you what little girls are made of. Alaisja seemed pleased with our living situation. She had more time with me at home; I was available to do activities with my child. We especially like to paint and play dress up.

Alaisja was my guiding light. Light of the lighthouse that brought me in from the darkness or kept me from going too far into the deep. I was thankful for and showed her in every tangible way possible. I doted on her and she'd come to know it. My mother ensured my daughter was brought up with a strong Christian faith. I'd rarely attend church as I started reading books that questioned the existence of God as taught in the Christian faith. I never really imposed my views on my daughter, I allowed her grow in her own understanding providing real answers inquisitive questions.

Perry is Jamerican Rasta. This means he's an American with Jamaican heritage. Perry's mother was born in Douglas, GA and his father born to the Red Hills of Jamaica. Perry taught our daughter the value of her femininity as mandated through the eyes of Jah Rastafari. While I didn't agree with everything from the culture, I did appreciate the lifestyle and liberty of the Black Man and Black Woman. I leaned more to the Islamic teachings of God as I admired the Muslim. The dedication to Allah and the consistency of keeping holy within the body and without truly intrigued me. I was also impressed by Sunni Muslim theories regarding their understanding of the household hierarchy.

CHAPTER 14

Let's See What This New Life Be About

I'd stopped stripping and hustling to focus on getting my life together. I owed to Alaisja, she given this world without a choice in the matter. On the other hand, According to Lorna Byrne's book A Message of Hope from the Angels, Archangel Michael told her that a child chooses its parents before conception, while still a soul in heaven. Byrne claims that the child chooses its parents knowing everything about them, including their good and bad qualities, and chooses them over all others. I pray that the latter is true. Either way, Alaisja deserved better than having a street running mother. I have to at least try for her sake.

    I'd taken Shahada which is an Islamic oath and creed that is the first of the Five Pillars of Islam. It is an Arabic phrase that states, "I bear witness that there is no deity but God, and I bear witness that Muhammad is the Messenger of God". The Shahada is a sacred testament that Muslims are expected to uphold throughout their lives. It is recited at many important moments in a Muslim's life. The most beautiful thing that I heard was Surah Al-Qasas – 56, it teaches that God guides who He chooses. This meant that I did not choose Islam, God chose me. That was love to me and that is what I needed love. Nobody gets too much love any love anymore. Compassion is becoming a lost characteristic.

    I feel in the love with the teachings of the Prophet Muhammad. Islam resonated with the lost voice on the inside of me. I needed this discipline. I learned so much about myself, about my body, about my soul. The importance of living a righteous life before God. Why was I essential to God's plan? I learned the ordained purpose of a household. It was all love, peace and elevation. I made sure to make my prayers five times a day. I changed my nutritional diet according to Halal and Haram. I'd become a devout Muslimah. I wore my an-abaya and proudly covered my head. I even wore niqab, which is a veil or long garment worn by some Muslim women to cover their face and hair, but not their eyes.

I wore this attire around my family and was asked by a toddler if I was a darn Ninja! I laughed so hard and explained to his little mind that I was Muslim. He tried to understand by rationalizing the clothing with that of a little a girl that was in his class. I advised him to befriend her and to not make fun of her. He made a promise to me in which he'd kept. Mashallah (God willed it).

Living as a Muslim was an adjustment for my entire family. My grandparents were the first to accept me without bias after they say that was serious about my deen. My deen can be define as a system of life where Almighty Allah (SWT) is worshipped and obeyed, not just in the narrow religious sense, but in a manner that includes all aspects of human life. I come from an Ol' Southern family that cooked with lard, fat back, salted pork, bacon grease; we even ate chitterlings. When I turned down a pot of my granny collard greens and fried ribs, everyone knew that I was serious. I kept the faith for time until one summer day in Florida I had to make a choice, put on hijab and sweat it out at the bus stop or put on something unrevealing but suited for the weather? I chose the latter.

I'd faltered on my deen. But the teachings of the Prophet Muhammed lived in my heart. It was hard for me not fully practicing. Until I met the gorgeous guy at the mall, 5'9" light-skinned with greens brother. He had my attention. When the brother approached me, I immediately lowered my gaze. He noticed! He stepped back and asked, "You're a Muslimah?" I softly replied, "Yes." The brother shouted, "Merciful Allah!" All in the middle of Regency Mall with was pretty lit at this period in time. That was so cute though.

The green eyed brother had a strong Arabic/Muslim name, Rakim. The meaning of Rakim is: A merciful person. Rakim was so peaceful and knowledgeable of all things Muslim. He was really on his deen and had sent his intentions for me in motion from the first moment we met. I liked him and all but I need to run this meeting by my appointed chaperone which was not there when Rakim and I met. He was cool with that; he respected me.

After leaving the mall, I'd stopped to pick Alaisja up from school. She and I took a nice stroll to the house as we talked about her day. She was such a cool toddler. We stopped by the neighborhood Dairy Queen for our usual caramel sundaes. We sat and for little while to eat our ice cream which allowed us to beat the Florida heat. That is only one of the many precious moments that I hold sacred as a first time mom.

We'd finished our ice cream and commenced our stroll. We pass a the local Block Buster and just as we got to the outside jewelry window of Kay's; I saw a set of white gold diamond earrings perfect for me my little girl. I paused and decided to walk into the store where by the favor God meet the presence of relative. To him, I was little Princess with her baby; he found that sweet. In the South, when an elder call you or a situation concerning you, sweet; the mean something other than the meaning of the actual word.

I'd introduced my relative to my baby girl and told that I wanted to purchase the diamond earrings in the window for her. He gave me a look of astonishment and oh la la. "Well, honey those over there (pause) where do you work?" I told him the information and he looked at me, "Princess, how you is now girl?" I told him. My relative looked me over once more and said, "You'd better go girl! Look at you, honey!" I smiled in appreciation. "Look see, I really want my baby to have those earrings today." He says, "Oh honey, we can do that. How much money do you got on you?" "I got fifty dollars," I'd said. My cousin snickered and said, "Baby, let me run your credit and see what we can do for you today."

Run my credit? What did he mean by that? I'd never heard such a phrase yet I was intrigued. My relative asked for my identifying information; which I provided. He did his thing on the computerized cash register. My relative, "Honey, you can get those earrings and some mo'!" "Girl, what else do you see in here you want for your baby?" I looked around and noticed that the store wasn't quite toddler friendly. Sooo, I saw a diamond ring that sat nicely in the showcase. "Let me see that ring right there." "Girl, you have good taste. I know we family, girl!" I tried on the diamond ring and it fit nicely. That was the first time, I'd ever purchased anything on credit. My relative told me about the monthly payments but I was not aware of the consequences of not making *on-time* payments.

Alaisja and I hadn't made it cross the threshold of the house before I heard my momma annoyingly say, "I'm glad you home. Some damn boy name Kim or RaRa or some shit like that, don' called here for six damn times back to back." I just looked at her with a gaze which said *I don't want no problems, Momma*. "Princess, who in this is that? Tell him don't be calling people house like that. It rude as hell!" I dared not respond. I just went on about my business which was tending to my daughter. I got to that real quick because I didn't need marching orders from her at that point.

I gave Alaisja her bath for the evening and we ate dinner. After dinner, she and I sat down to go over her colors. The color *yellow* would always trick her up as she'd inherited a speech impediment from her father. I didn't let that stop me from teaching her how to enunciate her words. After going over letters, we prepared for bedtime (for her not me). After she was snug and sound asleep. I decided to ask my mom if Rakim had left a number. Momma gave me a look that would turn Medusa into stone. My stepdad got a kick out of that and told my momma to give me the number and she did.

I called Rakim that night and we talked for hours or should I say he taught for hours. What stood out to me was the fact that Rakim was just getting out of prison. I knew people who had gone to prison and knew some that had gotten out of prison. However, I'd never dated either of those persons. When Rakim told me what he'd gone to prison for and how it all happened, my heart went out to him.

You see Rakim was a thirteen year old black male who'd recently moved to Jacksonville, Florida from the burgs of California. One night, Rakim along with a group of his friends decided that were going to miss their curfew because they wanted to go to their neighborhood corner store to get some candy. This night, the young black boys decided to take the long way which was along the train tracks where the boys saw what appeared be an injure person. As the boys got closer, they noticed that the injured person was a dead pregnant woman. The boys ran to Rakim's mother's house which was the closet house to their location.

The boys told the mother what they'd found. Rakim's mother did the right thing by reassuring the boy and calling the police. The police arrived to the mother's house, questioned the young black boys and had the boys take them to where they'd saw the deceased. The boys did as ask. The two detectives arrived on the scene and asked the boys the damning question, "What were you boys during back here?" The kids were arrested on the scene. Later, the boys were all charged with the murder of the woman and her baby. They were sentenced. Rakim, went to jail at thirteen and released at the age of twenty-six. Funny thing, there were more women found dead in the same location for several years after the boy were arrested. *Either they don't know or don't care what happens in the hood.*

Rakim and I made a holistic go of things. It was hard for him to remain celibate after being imprisoned for half of life. He didn't want to pressure me into having sex before marriage so we got engaged. I wanted to marry Rakim. Even though we did not live together he provided for me and Alaisja. My family had grown fond of him which made living as a Muslim a lot easier and at home. Rakim didn't mind that I did not wear hijab, I was his intended. Rakim and I had a meeting of the minds which landed us on the same page. He understood that

I was not comfortable with the dynamic of having more than one wife. He didn't want to take care of more than one woman.

The question came in reference to my dowry. I knew Rakim's financial status as a black man in America with a record such as his. I'd decided that I wanted a set of Hadith. Hadith is a narration of the message as given to the Prophet Muhammed from Allah. Rakim was pleased and agreed to my dowry request. We on just fine until Rakim had the urge for intercourse. His frustration with his needs not met had started to take a toll on our relationship. Long story short, Rakim called off our engagement. Needless to say, I was devasted, pissed off and humiliated. Men and their ego, ugh!

Rakim and I remained friends but it had become very difficult for me to communicate with him. I was sore about the whole ordeal. While I did not love him, I'd trusted him with me. I trusted Rakim to keep his word. He'd let me down and I couldn't see him the same as before. Yet, we remained friends. I kept my faith until one Sunday afternoon while my family was at church. It was Ramadan which is a time for spiritual reflection, self-improvement, heightened devotion and worship. Ramadan lasts for 30 days when in which a Muslim must fast each day from sun up to sundown.

I was into my second week of Ramadan, fasting from sun up to sundown. I made salat each day as required; five prayers a day. Somewhere in between prayers and halaqa classes, I started to feel famished. Halaqa is an Islamic study session similar to Christian Bible Study. This particular halaq targeted the ways and requirements of a Sunni Muslimah. Moving forward, this particular Sunday afternoon, my grandparents had cook Sunday dinner before everyone went off to church. Bar-b-que pork ribs, collard greens with salt pork, white rice and hot water cornbread was the dinner. I was famished, remember? I ate all of the ribs, half the pot of greens and all of the hot water cornbread. That moment I'd decided that I no longer had the discipline to continue the Muslim walk of faith.

When my family returned home, I was in my bed sleeping like Goldilocks after eating the three bears' porridge. I woke to Alaisja's hand on my face and her soft voice saying, "Momma, ma, momma." I replied, "Yes, Lay-Lay." I could hear the commotion of voices and movements as I came to. Slow motion, I put on house slippers and walked to the front of the house.

Grandfather: "Got dayum Princess, you ate all that food like that?" "We thought the food was safe because you Muslim."

Grandmother: "Looks like she ain't Muslim no mo'. "God do answer prayers."

Mother: "Girl, I told you that you wasn't no damn Muslim."

Brother: "I'm glad, 'cause she was tripping for real for real!"

Stepdad: Snickering in the corner.

Grandfather: "Don't be shame babygirl! Hell, you was hungry. You still hungry, baby?"

Family: "Her ass bet' not be hungry after she don' ate all that food!"

Me: "Well, I'm sorry ya'll"

Mother: "I told everybody you was going through an identity crisis."

CHAPTER 15

Crazy, Sexy, Cool

I guess all of that fasting and clean eating had done my body good. I was fit as Equine Ethologists' best Mare; a brick house and then some. I'd jumped back in game but no longer in the strip clubs. I remember the plan that was presented to me way back when Killer Joe told me about those AIDS pills. Times were still difficult for African countries and certain parts of Haiti to receive the proper medications needed to treat the disease. I'd figured that I could make a slight profit, all while helping others. I mentioned this plan to my cousin; the same cousin that supplied my cocaine. He wasn't sold on the idea so I called Kirk. Kirk was with it and the game commenced. Kirk was actually shocked to see me unlocked and loaded.

I had homegirls that didn't know a thing about my operations with the exception of my white homegirl Liz. Liz was a real street runner. Liz came true every time and never spoke about our business. My other homegirls were tricks, pill poppers and club hoppers; I loved them but they didn't love me. Later on life I found that none of them chicks I hung with except Liz were loyal. Darn shame too; because I still got love for them... it's just different.

One night out with my homegirls, I ran into Rakim. He was now a bouncer at the hottest nightclub in the city. I locked eyes with him but he didn't recognize me. I walked over to him and tapped his shoulder, "As-salamu alaykum Rakim." He turned swiftly yet slowly, "Princess?" Rakim's green eyes sparkled in the night lights. "Princess, what do you have on? I've never seen you like _this_ before!" I had on a form fitting low neckline revealing my ample bosom, black dress that came upon my knees. High heeled shoes, skin glistening, no blemishes and well oiled. Hair down the small of my back and layered to accentuate my cheek bones; thanks to my kidnapper for showing me how to see me.

I basked in Rakim's attraction to me. I spoke with definitive intentions to lure him in just to let him down. I hugged Rakim and seductively walked away. His gaze was upon for the rest of the night. As I exited the club, Rakim found me and started explaining his decision for calling of our engagement. I was disappointed in him yet again. It took for him to see me dressed like that to see me; what a jerk! I told him that I forgave him and walked away. Vindication!

The rhythm of the night got me caught up yet again. I was a club hopper and I loved it. I love to dress up and fix my hair. Pretty clothes, the latest tunes, alcohol, money, time, sex for authority never pleasure, it was liberating. I woke in the morning rushing through the day just to get to the night. My new found friend Zhane came into my life at the right time for the both us. We were both single moms with daughters the same age and we were 2 days apart in birth. We clicked.

Zhane needed more money than what she making at her day job in retail. She was introduce to me by my Aunt with whom she worked with. Kirk didn't like Zhane. He called her low-down dirty filthy the first day he'd met her. While I was appalled by what Kirk called, Zhane found it funny. I should've known then something wasn't right about her. It took twenty of friendship to find out that Zhane never liked me. Anyway, upon meeting Zhane I heard her story and figured I could show her around the strip club. That's what she wanted to do so why not.

I told Zhane about a new club that was closer to our home and that I'd heard it was a hot spot. I told Zhane that she would need to start to during the week in order to secure a spot for the weekend rotation. The schedule didn't conflict with her work hours during the day so she was with it. I told her to be to my house that following Tuesday by 7:00pm. That girl was on time. I heard two knocks at my door and when I opened the door, I saw a video vixen! "Ok Ok Ok, come on in, girl and make yourself at home." Zhane heard me in my bathroom trying to get my hair to cooperate with the style I was intending. She walked in said, "Let me do it." That girl had the hands of Midas himself. When I got done and it didn't take her long, my intended style didn't hold a candle to what she'd achieve. From that point on she became my hair stylist. No one can do my hair like she does. Shame that I lost her as a friend and stylist. Such as life.

We made our way to Sensations, which was the name of the strip club. Zhane was allowed to work that night but she was a little nervous. I bought her two shots of vodka and she lit for the rest of the night. The club owners liked her style and hustle, so they gave her their blessing to work there. Zhane made so much money that night. At first, everyone thought it was because she was the new face in the building. We all later found out why. You see Zhane had a pimp who had been her high school Math teacher. She was a familiar face from other scenes which made her time at Sensations less competitive.

I liked that girl, why did have to be a trick. I tried to convince her to stop tricking by explaining to her that she was a prostitute. She told me to mind my business and that I did for that moment on. Zhane was a real go getter, she didn't let the grass grow under her feet for nothing. I admired her because although we partied and hustled; Zhane had real goals. Goals that surpassed her current situation and she went for it.

The life had started to take its toll on me yet again. My mother had grown deeply concerned about my lifestyle and my role as a parent. I took care of Alaisja but she didn't like what she thought I did to take care of her. My mother would preach to me about changing how I lived. I didn't want to hear it until I got robbed at gunpoint three buildings away from where my child was. The entire time the pump was pressed to the back of my head all I could think about was my baby girl and my momma. I started to pray.

The guy with the gun to my head heard me praying. "Yo' man, she over here praying!" The accomplice says, "Bitch, shut up before he soot your dumb ass!" I replied, "Look what the hell ya'll want? You already got everything; ain't shit else to get." I could feel the guy with the gun to head shaking, which caused the gun to shake. I prayed, "Lord, please don't this gun off. Please don't let me die like this." I heard a voice say, "You shall live and not die…" I knew it wasn't the voice of the robbers. I think to myself, *who was that?*

The guy with the gun to head commanded me to get on the ground. I told him no and explained to him that I wasn't going to let him hurt me. He whispered in my ear, "Baby, I ain't no killer or no rapist but my homeboy is crazy. Please just do as I ask." I complied with his instructions. Before I knew it, the robbers were gone, and I was still alive unharmed. Broke but alive.

When I realized that the coast was clear, I got up and went straight to the apartment where my daughter and mother were. I didn't tell anyone what happened to me. I simply hugged my mother ever so tightly and held my daughter ever so closely. I had to make a change.

The next day, I called Liz and told her to meet me at my house. Liz should up with her kids and baby daddy in the car. She called me to announce that she had arrived and was waiting outside. I told her to come in and she did. I sat down with Liz and told her what happened to me. She was on revenge and I was told her that I hadn't seen the faces of the robbers. I gave Liz all of the dope that I had in my possession. I paid her what was owed to her and ended that part of my life for good.

Now, what was I going to do, I still didn't have a formal education, my skills were limited and bills were due. I saw an ad in the newspaper for a job fair. It had been a while since I needed a resume but I knew I needed one. I went to the area library and found a book on resumes and interviewing tactics. I sat the computer and drafted my resume using the format from the book. I brushed up on my interview skills using the methods for the other book. One my way home, I stopped by Kmart to buy clothes fitting for an interview. I'd purchased a pair of black slacks, a white button blouse, stockings and a pair of three inch close toe pumps. I was ready for the job after printing off ten copies of my resume.

The day of job fair, I'd gotten dressed, pulled my hair into a neat bun secured by chopsticks, a dash of white diamonds and pearl stud earrings. I caught the bus to the location as by this time, I still did not know how to drive. I entered the building and realized the competition was thick. I wasn't intimidated just aware that I needed to bring my A-game. There were many job seekers and just as my many recruiters. I was in the kitchen and had to cook. I saw two recruiters in the back of all of the others and made my way to them. They were eager to greet me as they hadn't had much traction due to their location.

"Hi, my name is Princess Booker," I said as I extended my hand to shake theirs. They return the sentiment and for my resume. Each of them took a gander was somehow impressed. I'd lied on my resume about my education and embellished a lot regarding my work experience. I sold skills that I didn't know I had and they bought it. "When can you start?" That was music to my ears. I'd secured a temporary position with a staffing agency with weekly pay and an hourly wage of $15.00 an hour! I was on cloud nine.

I worked the temp position for ninety days until I was offered a permanent position. I pounced. I was ecstatic. My mother was off my back and my daughter had more time with her mom. I was home cooking meals and helping my daughter grow into the fabulous woman she is today. Life was good but the struggle got real. I needed more money. I didn't let the pressures of living this *new life* turn me around. I took on an overnight shift working at a fast food restaurant making minimum wage. I didn't complain one bit. I'd worked two jobs for almost a year. I was able to build a small savings, hang with my homegirl Zhane and take small day trips when I had a day off.

Life started to pan out a bit for ya girl. One day, I ran into a guy that I grew up with. He was just in town visiting family. The two of us were astonished at the moment as he'd move to the West Coast during our eighth grade year. We hung out the entire six weeks he was in town. It was pretty cool and I enjoyed his quirky humor. It was time for him to leave so we exchange good-byes. I never thought I'd see him again until a month later when I had to call to give the news of my pregnancy.

Neither of us were ready for that news! I felt it only fair to inform the man that I was now carrying his baby. That phone was distressing due to our silence. We didn't intended for this happen. We just wanted to lay and play for a bit, you typical grown people stuff. He asked how I was feeling. I told him that I honestly wasn't ready for another child. Then this man said, neither am I. He never told me that he had kid. Well, that was neither here nor there as we were at a crossroads where a life changing decision needed to be made. The call ended; my life didn't.

I didn't tell anyone about my pregnancy. I could hear my mother's voice had I'd given her the news and that is not what I needed. I sat on the sofa in my living room, contemplating my life as a mom. To raise two kids with no money wasn't fair to me nor was it fair to me. I stood up from the sofa and walked into my bedroom, where I stood in front of my mirror. Look at me, I cannot have another baby right now. My body will be messed up. Well, that African told me that I could have up to six children without losing my figure. But, how do I know if he was right? He looked at the hips of a twelve-year-old girl and determined her maternal fate. Lord, I am losing myself. All of this ran my mind wild; I needed a glass of wine. Ahhh damn, I can't drink! What am I going to do?

Alaisja and I woke up this following for morning. As we walked hand in hand to her bus stop, we chatted a bit. I turned to her and asked how would you feel if mommy was pregnant? She didn't respond verbally but the look on her confirmed that I was having the wrong conversation with this child. So, we continued to the bus stop in silence. As we stood there, I noticed a few of the women were standing waiting with multiple children. Some faces looked tired, the others were worn. I didn't want to wear either of those faces. The bus finally arrived and I slowly walked away once I saw Alaisja securely seated. As I walked back towards my place, my knees buckled and I starting violently vomiting. In my mind, I thought *there is no way that I can do this*. A small petite woman walked over to me and placed her hand on my back, "Baby, you're pregnant huh? I see you every morning with your little girl? How old are you? You're gonna be alright." After I gathered my bearings, I thanked the woman for her failed attempt to comfort me.

I am not having this baby! I called my old friend and told him that I didn't want to have this baby. He listened and said not a word as I ranted about life and my fears that my life would be with another kid. "Hey are you there? Can you hear me, fool?" "Princess, I ain't no fool but what we've done was definitely foolish. I can't handle having a child right now, especially a child that would live so far away from me. I would want to be a part of that child's life and right now I wouldn't be able to do that." I paused and realized that he'd been thinking about this too. This situation was not only about what I wanted, it was kid too! That would be fair to just determine how I was going to proceed in this situation without giving this man a voice in the matter; this was his child and mine.

The conversation went on without an end just a goodbye. Solemnly, I went about my days. Full of uncertainty and imbalance, I received my first write-up, reprimanding me for not following protocol which was totally out of character for me. I had to figure something out. The guy kept calling my phone but I did not answer. Finally, I decided to listen to his voicemail messages. There was one that caught my heart, "Princess, I know you're scared, but if you choose to keep the baby, I will be its father. I will provide for my child and you. But, whatever you decide is best for you and your daughter, I will accept." I was crushed and touched at the same time. I decided to pray and ask God to show me the right thing to do. I received and answer but I didn't listen as I didn't know it was God…until!

I had an abortion! Even though the facility had given me drugs to numb me and put me to sleep; I could feel everything and I could hear everything. I could feel the suction of the vacuum pull my baby from body. I could hear my baby's bones break. I could hear the nurse as she performed the procedure, crying. When I was fully awake, my body felt empty… hallow. I couldn't believe what I'd done. I killed my baby! What kind of person am I? Would God forgive me for this? Would I forgive myself? This memory never goes away. Sometimes, I think my baby visits me each year around his would have been birthday. I even thought I saw his spirit one night standing at the end of my bed; that's how I know it was boy. At that time, he would have been five years old. Aborting my baby is one of the two life decisions I would regret for the rest of my life.

CHAPTER 16

I couldn't cope after having that abortion. I needed an escape from the thought of that damning day. The only thing I knew that helped to free my mind was weed; marijuana. I needed a blunt and silence. She's bacccck... they say old habits die hard but they never tell you why. I didn't want to party like a rock star but I sure as hell needed an affiliation of the sort. I mean, I had to keep my job and the level of independence I'd acquired fit me. I had by business attire on one side of the closet and my freak'um dresses on the side. I traded glasses of Chardonnay for shots of Hennessy. Long walks in the park were replaced with small cyphers of smoke in the air. Lois Lane by day and Vanity 6 by night; more masks. Let's not forget my faithful sidekick Zhane. She was excitesd to see me back in the action. I didn't go too far but I met the line.

Nobody told me that life would have so many hills, valleys, mountains, storms, dry places and many rivers to cross. I wasn't happy but I wasn't sad either, I guess the term that I'm looking for is euthymic mood. Euthymic mood is a state of okayness which could easily become a psychological problem. I stayed in this mood for too long as life went on and later needed a Psychologist to help me shake through it. I had feelings of greatness and nothingness all at the same. To see yourself living a life of tranquility, financially liberated, beautiful and put together but not believing that you'll ever be able to obtain it. Waking up to life had started to become a real chore; bills, crisis after crisis, let down after let down all drowned by the Purple Haze, kept afloat by the glamour of a Mai Tai.

Looking at the face of my daughter reminded me that I wasn't good enough to be her mother. I didn't stop trying; I fought against my emotions and went hard every day to give her what she wanted and needed. I couldn't fail her even though I'd failed myself. Life was no longer about me, I constantly reminded myself of this. She deserves the utmost! So I would wear masks whenever needed to appear what I needed to be, which had a greater purpose… her life over mine.

Sweeping my front porch, I met the look upon me from this black ass dude. Cordially, I waived good day and he nodded his head from to return my gesture. I looked up and again and there he was still staring at me. *Why is this fool staring at me for? Get a life, nigga damn.* Those were my thoughts at the time. I hated when someone would stare at me. It made me feel anxious as if they were plotting on me. It still does but the anxiety isn't as bad now. After sweeping my front porch, I'd decided to walk to the corner to get me a couple of Garcia Vegas and a few Debbie Cakes (the Zebra kind). On my way home from the store, I walked through the nature path, which was also an ally for homeless drug addicts and prostitution acts, and saw that same black ass dude in the middle of transactions. I looked him and he looked at me; I shook my head to let him I was displeased and don't even try to talk to me. You know this Negro smiled at me! But he had the whitest teeth and a boyish grin.

Home now, it was time to close out the noise while Alaisja played in her room. I turned my radio and popped in a Maze featuring Frankie Beverly CD. The velvet voice of art that came from Frankie, the perfected percussions, woodwinds, high brass and battery brought joy to my soul that lightened the mood in my home. I sparked my spliff and inhaled the potency of THC which balanced my ADHD, sipped on my coffee and two-stepped across my floor. Ahhhh, there it was a glimpse of happiness.

Here comes the rain again, my mother knocking at my door just to remind me that the wages of my sins were death. She intentionally entered my home with her left foot knowing how I'd felt about that. That was one of the Muslim teachings that I'd taken with me as if signified one's respect for you and your home. Nevertheless, my mom stood in my living room and admired my new decorations. She bopped her head a bit to the music playing in the background and asked me what I'd cooked for the day.

"Momma, I'm cooking oxtail soup today. With jalapeno cornbread."

"O' you've figured out how to make my oxtail soup?" My mother asked with an approving grin.

"Yes ma'am. I know just how to make too, Momma."

We made our way to the sofa where we sat and she told me all about my brother, who was incarcerated in Texas at the time. I gave my mother two hundred dollars to put on my brother's books and ensured her that she would have that from every other Friday until he was home. We talked a little more before he started telling me about a *nice young man* she knew. She felt like this *nice young man* would be good for me and Alaisja. I was not down for that. I could not stand people wanting to fix me up with someone. I can find my own man. I wasn't very successful at it by checking my track record; but I was capable of finding my own man!

My mother sat there raving about this *nice young man*. He helps the older women in her neighborhood with their groceries. He stops by from time to time to check on her and if she needs her trash taken out; he would that as well. I listened as best as I could be her words started to sounding like *BLAH BLAH BLAH*! "Ok Ma, check it out, I will start going to church with but it won't be every Sunday." I was not ready to settle down, I have Alaisja and that was enough unless it was with Kirk. I'd kept my promise to my momma and started attending church; not often, but I was there.

After several church services and more time with my family. The thought of settling down started to sound more like something I could try. Kirk wasn't coming around anymore and that left me wanting. I would reserve my soul for Kirk but seek an alternate since he'd decided not to choose me. So, I called Zhane to talk to her about my broken heart and to get her thoughts on me moving on; you know, girl talk. By this time, Zhane had become engaged to one of her tricks so life was good for her. "Princes, are you serious crying about the nigga? Girl, he ain't even that cute for real. You can definitely do better. I was wondering when you were going to wake up!" I laughed with humility and surprise. I knew that Zhane didn't like him but dang,

A few months had gone by and I went over to my momma's house for dinner: salmon croquettes, Roger Wood sausage and hominy grits. After convincing Alaisja to that the salmon croquettes were the Krabby Patties from her beloved cartoon SpongeBob; I absorb lively conversation with my family and a hearty meal. Life felt simple in that moment.

My mother had gone into her bedroom and I followed her. I plopped myself down on her bed and she looked at me, "Princess, you okay?" I was okay just needed to talk to my momma. While I relationship was as commercially advised on Disney, she was my rock. My momma's presence always reminded to tough it out and go forward. I looked at momma as she did what she was doing, I didn't pay attention as I was trying to figure out how to ask her about that *nice young man* she'd told me about. I the words finally shot of my mouth, "Momma, what happened to that *nice young man* you'd told me about. She looked back at over with a show of inquisition and said, "Girl, I know you playing. Oh, now you want to meet me him. I thought you didn't need not help with finding a man." She told me more about the *nice young man* and this time she had my attention.

My mother schedule a time for me to the *nice young man*. I wasn't nervous but shocked when he arrived to my momma's house. "Momma, stop playing with me," I'd asked. "Girl, what's your problem?" Honey, the *nice young man* was the black ass dude that I'd saw staring at me while sweeping my porch. I was disappointed to say the most. The black ass dude introduced his black ass self and I reciprocated. My momma left the room, giving the illusion of privacy as if she wasn't somewhere listening.

The black ass guy and I decided to take a walk outside as it was below freezing inside my momma's house. He was actually pretty cool to talk to. We found out that we had few things in common with the exception of smoking weed. We bonded over our drug habit and somehow made a baby. I'd made a baby with the black as dude that had previously creeped me out. He and I became friends and lovers or as should I say intimate lovers and friends. Until I got pregnant. His true colors started to shine through quite brightly. But the black ass dude had won me over. Did I love him? Nah, just desperate enough to settle.

There's this saying, "Sometimes you can stay in a place too long." I was with the black ass dude too long honey. Before the pregnancy, you couldn't keep his black ass away from me. He would want to be wherever I was and do whatever it was that I was doing. At first it was cool but then I started to question his motives. For instance, how was it that he always had money without a job or a hustle? I mean in the beginning I'd realized that he was a corner hustler. You are the nickel and dime type…crumbs no bricks wife beater wearing black as nigga type dude. I didn't judge him or nothing as I wasn't looking to be with this black ass dude for real. He was a placeholder until Kirk came to his senses or whatever. Plus, he was good company ya' know. He made me laugh and he also prayed. I used to have this really bad abdomen pain. I'd gone to the doctor about it but they couldn't find any cause for the pain. I'd lived with that pain for some time until one day I had a bad episode in front of the black ass dude. I'd fallen to the living room floor with beads of sweat lingering on my forehead; groaning in pain. The black ass dude wasn't scared but jumped in to action. "Princess, you straight?" Why would he ask me that; like come on. Clearly, I was not straight!

I made my way from the floor to the sofa with his help. His eyes had so compassion for me in that moment. I could see something good in him. He placed his left hand to my forehead and his right hand on my tummy, he recited the ninety-first Psalms in entirety. I was impressed. He began to pray God for my healing and better health. From that day on, I have never felt that pain again. After that, I'd figured that I should let him in a bit; I removed one of my masks. The mask of manipulation was retired for the moment.

It was something that he was keeping from me but I couldn't put my finger on it. We'd slept together one night as we did many other nights before. However, this night was different. During intercourse, I didn't see him as himself; I saw something demonic. His face had changed. His lovemaking didn't feel sensational it felt weirdly uncomfortable. My bedroom was eerie like the moment stood still and all I could see was blood dripping from my walls. I wanted him off of me but he just looked at me as if he knew what I feeling and seeing. I paused in disbelief. As soon as he was done, I made him leave my house. I didn't talk to him for weeks until I found out that I was pregnant!

I've only shared this with one other person with is my Aunt Jolene. She was more spiritually well-rounded than I. When I told her my tale she had look of concern but I knew she believed me. She told me not worry and that God was with me. She then gave me her spiritual synopsis which was that, "…there are people out here that will put roots on you by sex with you. They do it for different reasons but girl, it's real." I listened to her but I did not want to believe that; even though a part of me totally believed it. I told her that I was never going to talk to him again. He'd scared me; that event freaked me out. She told me to read my Bible and to pray for God's protection. I heard her but I didn't do any of what she'd said.

A few days after speaking my Aunt Jolene, a little old lady name Ms. Caroline walked over to me as I stood outside chatting with a few of my neighbors. Ms. Caroline walked right over to me and interrupted our conversation, "Hey, pretty black child. Looks like you've met your match. For every lie, act of deception you've met a man that is about to best you. He's gonna take you up and down baby. But don't worry, God ain't gon' let him kill you. God gotta keep you alive for that baby in yo' stomach!" She smiled and walked off. I was so darn confused. I knew what she was talking about but I wasn't aware of a pregnancy. It was Ms. Caroline's prophesy that prompted me to take a pregnancy test. I took the test… it was positive.

CHAPTER 17

Ms. Caroline's Prophesy

I'd told the black ass guy the results of my pregnancy test was positive. He was happy and declared it would be a boy. I was happy as I'd convinced myself that the son I aborted was being reincarnated. Not even two months after receiving a positive confirmation from my doctor did I see a drastic change in the now father of my baby. He didn't come around much anymore and when he did he would always press me for information regarding my connections. I would explain to him that I no longer had street affiliations. He would get angry and accuse me of random stuff of like not wanting to see him succeed. That wasn't it at all, I just wasn't allow him to eat from my table as he was qualified.

The black ass dude all of sudden felt entitled to all things Princess; my body, my home, my food, my weed, my lane, my life. The audacity of this slum dog; and how the hell did I try myself like this. Drugs, depression, poverty, sex and untreated trauma do not mix. It is a recipe for ghetto love that I did not want but somehow found myself caught in a spider web not spawn by Charlotte. This black ass dude ran a circle around my life. He had gotten close up on my side hustle operations and tried to infiltrate my connects. I wouldn't let him so this frustrated that slum dog so much so that he'd set me up. On account of the fact that I would no longer allow him to my home; the black ass dude decided that he would call me and entice me with money for the baby. I took the bait.

I'd caught a cab to the Eastside of Jacksonville where the slum dog and his cronies lived. I arrived at his grandmother's house. I went and sat on the woman's porch awaiting his arrival. The slum dog pulled up in a clean white vehicle, skinnin' and grinnin' as if to impress me. I wasn't impressed at all. I just wanted the money he'd promised. It's not like I needed it but I was carrying his child. He got of the car and asked me to take a ride with him to discuss our relationship. What relationship was the fool talking about? Honey, I asked him where he'd gotten the car from before stepping foot into the vehicle. It was tax season and I was pretty sure the car belonged to his other baby momma. I got in the car, nevertheless.

We drove a few blocks through his neighborhood while he complimented my pregnant glow. He was trying to mack me but I wasn't giving him no play. When he realized his rap wasn't making no noise, he changed the topic back to my side hustle. I wasn't trying to hear it and asked him to drop me off at the nearby community college campus. I was over his presence. Just then, I heard police sirens and saw the lights. We were being pulled over.

The cops pulled us over and searched the vehicle. Immediately a female cop arrived on the scene and began to frisk me. She didn't find anything on me. However, the found crack cocaine under my seat. I was handcuffed and placed in back one of the officer's cars. I sat there as the officers chatted outside the vehicle with the slum dog. He was then placed in the back seat of the vehicle with me. I was silent until I looked over and saw him in tears. The black ass dude was crying, are you kidding me? "Nigga, why are crying?" I asked. He responds, "I don't wanna go to jail! I can't go to jail man." He went to rambling in about stuff he had no business saying let alone saying it in the back of a police of car.

Needless to say, we were delivered and booked into the county jail. This was crazy as hell. I knew I shouldn't have went to meet this bad luck black ass dude. There we were in holding. Me with the women and him with the men. My name was called for pictures and fingerprinting afterwards I was returned back to the pool of women in lock up. My name was called again to see the nurse for weight and health check where I told the nurse that I was in my first tri-semester to pregnancy. After my visit with the nurse, a female cop assigned to escort me back to lock up, felt the need to wrangle me around. I asked her to not be so rough because I was pregnant. The officer laughed and commenced to manhandle me. I didn't resist at all; I just asked her to stop because I was pregnant. The woman said to me, "That's what you hoes always say!" I replied, "I don't know what them hoes be saying but bitch I am pregnant." The lady slammed me against the wall and handcuffed me. There were other officers witnessing this foolery and no one stopped her. I fell to my knees in pain. The female officer walked over to me grabbed me up by my upper arm and threw me into a single man holding cell. I was on the ground bleeding and crying, I was about to lose my baby.

I screamed so loud and I could hear the black ass guy yelling, "Bitch, what you did to my baby momma! Hoe I promise I will kill you if you did something to my baby momma!" This alarmed a male officer so much so that he opened the door to the cell I was in and saw the blood. He immediately called for a medic. The nurses came and you can see the sorrow in their faces. I heard a female voice say, "She really is pregnant. That girl told her she was pregnant."

I guess, I'd passed out because when I woke up, I was handcuff to a hospital bed hooked up to monitors. A cop stood guard of my room door as if I was some fugitive or an American Most Wanted suspect. The attending doctor was furious at my condition and demanded that I be uncuffed during my treatment. The officers on duty denied the doctor's request. At any rate, the doctor stopped the bleeding and saved my baby.

Upon returning back to the county jail, my momma had bonded me out so I was released shortly. But it wasn't before they served me that watery spaghetti that I did eat. Since I was pregnant, I was given two trays of food. I gave the other one away. Getting out of that place was all of I could think about. *Booker, pack it up!* Upon my release, I was given a court date. Failing to appear who have put my butt back in jail. I went to court and was given probation. Upon completion of my probation, my charges would be adjudicated.

The week after court, I went to check in at the probation office. I was assigned a female officer which did not play the radio. She defined the guidelines and advised me to strictly adhere to my sentence. Should I not, I would be back in jail. She saw that I was pregnant and asked, "So, you were locked up with your baby daddy huh?" I did not respond because she was trying to be funny and didn't hear a joke. My probation officer then said, "So, you stick with him, huh? Then read this!" I didn't know what she was talking but took a look at the paper in front of me. It was handwritten statement of account outlining all of my tea. Signed by the black ass dude! I couldn't believe it. The officer saw the look on my face and grinned. I didn't read anything funny on that document nor did I see anything around me that was funny. I was pissed off. I hated him! This dude tried to ruin my life. Thank God I had no prior drug convictions and the judge was extremely lenient. Thank God for favor, which I didn't know I had at the time.

My pregnancy was easy like my last one. I was sick all the time. My hair had started to fall out. I was taking my prenatal vitamins but I just couldn't keep anything I would eat down. I'd lost so much. I was hospitalized for dehydration. I didn't know if I was going to make it. So, I started talking to the baby a little more than usually. I would read the baby books and sing the theme song from the popular children's show, Lamb Chops. The baby seemed to like that; we were finally bonding.

Now eighteen weeks into my pregnancy, I find out my baby's gender. A boy! Immediately, I started to pray to ask God to cover my son. Cover him as a he would be a black male in American. Cover him from the sins of his parents. Make him gorgeous! Make him smart and strong. I knew he would be beautiful because as soon as the doctor told I was having a boy, I envisioned Shaka Zulu. That would be his name, Ishaka! Yep, Ishaka Toussaint. Ishaka after the legendary African Warrior Zulu King and Toussaint after the Great Haitian

Revolutionary Toussaint L'Ouverture. I admired the legacies of those men and was honored to name my son for them.

I was so happy to get to my momma's house to give my good news! As I entered the door exclaiming, "Momma, it's a boy!" Alaisja walked up to me, "Momma that black guy here." That child didn't say that but that's what I heard. I was crushed, but the he comes racing towards me, "Princess, we having a son?" *We?* No way man... I did not make this black ass dude the father of my SON! Such is life. What kind of mother would I be if I did not attempt to foster some sort of relationship with this fool. He wasn't good for me but maybe he'll be a decent dad.

Things didn't get crazy until the day I was due to delivery my son. In so much pain, the doctor's had given me morphine to carry me through. The morphine not only calmed the pain but it made me drowsy. I laid in the bed awaiting the time to come being visited by family and friends wishing us well. Then in comes, his black ass along with his sweaty friends and cousins. They were all wasted which disrupted my whole mood. As laid in the bed dealing with my emotions. He walks over and leans in close whispering in my ear, "You'll never get away from me. I own you now!" I felt a slap across my face so hard, I screamed. I couldn't fight back due the damn medicine. His cousin beckoned him to leave me alone and to leave the hospital. He listened to his cousin and left. I rejoiced! But, I couldn't wait to get out that hospital so I could kick his...

Hour later, my baby boy was born. Ishaka Toussaint Canty is his name. He was soooo darn handsome. He didn't cry much, he just looked at me like he knew exactly who I was. We gazed upon one another, getting to know each other. I held him close to me. As I held my baby boy in my arms, I prayed giving thanks to God for his life. I'd asked God to make his journey lite. He was so precious. In walks his dad, this time humbled and alone. He apologized for slapping me and asked to his boy. I didn't hesitate and placed Ishaka in his arms. I'll never forget that moment as I've never seen him like that again.

The arrival home was great! I was welcomed in love by all of my family and friends. My mother helped me out so much! Alaisja was old enough to pitch it as well; she'd blossomed into gorgeously smart little girl. She so was pleasant and strong. My babies, they were my dream to come true. No matter the situation, they were mine and I loved them. I needed them. Things were going so well. I'd forgotten how annoying the black ass guy was. He was so good with Ishaka. I didn't have to do very much for the baby when he was around. He would even help Alaisja with her Math homework from time to time. I'd removed another mask. The mask of indifference.

I had let this guy in not as a mate but as a friend. The phone rung, it was Kirk! Where had he been? Oh no, how am I going to tell him about Ishaka? He's going to be so disappointed. I didn't answer his call. However, later that night when the house was quiet; I returned his call. That was the most needed conversation as well as the saddest. You see, I'd thought Kirk had abandoned; moved on to something better. The entire time he was incarcerated. I didn't know. Now, here goes the sadness; "Kirk, I had a baby boy." He silence was chilling. "Princess, congratulations! When can I see him?" I couldn't believe that he wanted to see my son.

I gave Kirk the address to my place and he actually showed up. I wasn't quite living lavishly but it was a modest 2 bedroom. My goodness Kirk was so handsome; just like I'd met him but modified by the era. I welcomed him into my home, we sat and talked a bit before asked for Alaisja. Alaisja came running out of room with excitement to see Kirk. They hugged as he admired her growth. Kirk asked Alaisja to get her brother; she did just that. Alaisja placed Ishaka into Kirk's accepting arms. He held my baby boy as if he were his own. You could see the longing in his eye; the wish that Ishaka were his and mine. Time never allowed for us to procreate but our passion lives on.

Kirk left that evening leaving my heart in pieces. It seemed as if time stood still once again in my life. The tragedy of having a baby with the black ass due was a cost that I'd never knew I'd have to pay but indeed I did. I loved my baby boy but his father grieved my soul. Because I did not want to be with him, the black ass dude tortured me. Once, he set my front yard on fire, because I did not give him access to my body. I did allow visits for him and Ishaka, but he wanted more.

As Ishaka grew, the black ass dude antics increased. There was this one time when he broke into my house while I slept. Have you ever been asleep and woke up because you felt like it was someone in the room with you. Well, that happened to me but someone was actually in my room standing at the foot of my bed; it was the black ass dude. I panicked, that fool was seriously standing at the foot of my bed with a sick smile on his… watching me. I could not believe my eyes. He just stood there! "I told you, you'll never be free of me." He said as he turned and exited my bedroom. I sat there waiting for what I didn't know and still don't. I heard him go into my kitchen. I eased out of bed and walked towards him. This black ass dude was in there making a sandwich with a glass of sweet tea. Silence… he gathers his snack and leaves out of the back door.

A few days later, I got a call from the black ass dude asking for a visit with Ishaka. He wanted to take him to see some of his family members. I agreed. I was trying to co-parent despite the sadistic behaviors. When he arrived, I had Ishaka ready to go. As they left the house, I heard a faint whisper, "I might not ever bring him back, bitch!" I paused and chose not to over react. This was just his way of trying to antagonize me. I chose to ignore his statement. Big mistake.

Hours went by, they did not show up. I attempted to call his phone; no answer. I had my mother take to me his house; he didn't live there anymore. What was happening? I called his phone a thousand times; NO ANSWER! Where's my baby? He took him away from me. Day's had gone by before, my home phone rang. "Hello?"

"Yeah Bitch, I ain't never bringing him home. Imma kill ya' bitch and raise our son on top of your grave!" I couldn't believe this was happening to me. I called the police just for them to show up and tell me that it was nothing that they could without a court order. The father has just as many rights as the mother unless the court says otherwise.

I was without my son for an entire month all while receiving threatening phone from his dad. My Godsister Quana had come to visit me as she'd heard the news. She knew how I wasn't well due to the circumstance. Quana heard the house phone ring and decided to answer. She heard, "Shhh Shhhh Bitch Imma Kill You," followed by heavy breathing. That was the first time someone other than myself had heard the threats. Quana was deeply disturbed, so much so she cried and screamed at the top of her lungs, "This is Quana boy, you need stop playing and bring Ishaka home! This is not funny!" I'd heard all of it and came to the phone, "Please just bring him home. I will do whatever you want me to do. Just bring him home." Quana cringed at my begging, "Sistah, you ain't gonna do whatever he want you to do! Get his ass here and we gonna show him that ain't nobody about to play with you like this!"

A week later, my son was home. I was sitting in my living room watching *Friday After Next*, there was knock at the door. "Who is it?" I asked. There was no answer. I opened my front door and there was my child; sitting lively in his car seat looking up at me. No one else was there; just my son! I grabbed him up so quickly and exhaled as it seemed as though I hadn't breathed properly since he was taken. I thanked God all the day long. I called my momma and told her the news! She rushed over to my house as she couldn't believe it. Alaisja was so happy to have her brother home again. I allowed her to miss a few days of school just so that we were all home together.

As my house had gotten quiet after the welcoming of Ishaka. I sat stealthily in the dark contemplating how I was going to get rid of that black ass dude. There are hundreds of ways to kill a man; I chose one. The mask of seduction would work best for this situation. Then I figured out that this act would require more than one mask. I had to become a chameleon, comprised of deceit, seduction, manipulation and homemaker. An assassin! I had to get rid of his black ass. There was no way that I could let him live to continue his improper fun and games.

CHAPTER 18

Operation Assassin

I made nice with his black ass. I played the part of lover, friend and confidant. I even put up with his physical abuse to a certain extent. He would try to beat on him, but I knew how to protect myself which made it difficult for him to completely overtake me. One afternoon, he'd smacked me so hard my reflexes jumped into action. I'd grabbed the nearest object which happened to be an iron and hit him across his head. It dazed him but it didn't faze him. The sting of the iron caused him to stumble a bit while he grabbed his head. I didn't move as I was ready for whatever he wanted to bring. He didn't bring anything but a sigh with these words... *I love you, Princess.* I could not believe that this man had told me he loved me.

I stuck to the script and continued to disguise my disdained emotions. I was going to kill him but the timing had to be perfect. My homegirl Ladaana stopped by unexpectedly for a visit. He left us to our powwow. Ladaana and I chatted the afternoon away. I needed that sense of normalcy. I had a job but wasn't enthused enough to socialize with my co-workers. I just went in to work, did my duty and clocked out. Well most of the time, it was like that until I met Ladaana who wouldn't accept my silence. She was such a social butterfly. I appreciated her friendship because I was disgusted with my life at the time. Here I was with another child by a man who wasn't a man; fuck my life.

The black ass dude was horrible for me but very good with the kids. He was the one Alaisja depended on to assist her with her homework while I made dinner. He would spend time with Ishaka teaching him reading, writing and arithmetic. The dude wasn't dumb, he was just a fool. I appreciated the help but would gladly do without it if it had to come from him. We fought verbally and physically almost every other day. I grew tired of the need to sleep with one eye opened. I hated having to defend myself in my own home.

The time had come for me to reclaim my life. It was time to kill him. I called the black ass dude and invited him over for dinner. I'd enticed him with the promise of love making in his favorite positions. I also promised him that I wouldn't kick him out after. My mom had stop by to pick the kids for a few hours. That gave me time to set the scene. I'd cleaned my house from top to bottom, lit a few incense and allowed Calgon to take me away. I decided to read some pages in my Bible and came across Romans 12:19 *Do not take revenge, my dear friends, but leave room for God's wrath, for it is written: "It is mine to avenge; I will repay," says the Lord.*

Now, I read the scripture and understood clearly what it meant. However, I also understood that if this guy lived I would have to endure him until God saw fit to avenge me. That was torture just thinking about it. I'm killing him! After reading the scriptures, it was time for me to start dinner. Fried chicken wings, homemade mashed potatoes and gravy, fresh string beans and cornbread is what I prepared. I'd also made his favorite, my signature southern sweet tea. The kids were back home from their time with my mom. And, he'd arrived.

While I washed the kids up, I had a sidebar conversation with Alaisja advising her not drink the sweet tea. The tea was off limits. Alaisja didn't question me, she simply knew not to drink the sweet tea. Dinner was ready and the table was set. Everyone was eating, seemingly enjoying every bite. I smiled at my children now thinking about the *what if*. What if I get caught? What's going to happen to my children? Damn!

"Princess, didn't you say that you made sweet tea? Get me some, please."

I paused with the what ifs playing over and over in my mind. I pushed myself slowly from the table and made him a glass of sweet tea as asked. He scarfed down the full glass of tea and asked for another. I provided the second glass as asked. He chewed chicken and drunk tea, playing with the kids at the table. Then he mouthed something to me to keep the kids from hearing, that made the *what ifs* disappear from my mind, "Imma fuck the shit out'cha!" I couldn't believe I read his lips and that those were the words. My head was now back in the game. He's out of here no matter the consequences. Mask on!

I giggled at his jokes and swooned at his googly eyes. The children were done with their dinner. I washed them up and prepared them for bed. I tucked the kiddos in absorbing every minute with them as this could be the last time I would see them off to bed. I read them a story, which I'd made up as kid. They enjoyed that story a lot. My children fell asleep too fast this night. I wanted them to stay awake but also needed them to sleep.

Leaving the kids room, I made sure that their door was closed. I timidly walked into the living room to find his black ass sprawled across my sofa.

"Baby momma, that food was so damn good. You know you can cook! Can you make some tuna fish so I can have some for tomorrow?"

"Yeah, I can make some tuna. Let me put the rest of this food away and clean this kitchen."

"Girl, we can do that in the morning. Come on over here and watch t.v. with me. I haven't held you in a long time."

"No, let me get this kitchen cleaned up. I don't wanna wake up to dirty dishes."

"Ok then. Hurry up and while you're at make me another glass of tea."

This was now his fifth glass of tea. I handed him the full drinking glass of tea. He took a few sips. Just as I turned to go back into the kitchen, I heard the glass hit the floor and shatter. I paused and turned slowly to peep the scene. That black ass dude was out; he'd passed out.

I thought he was dead but he wasn't. I walked over to his body and felt for a pulse. I waited ten minutes and checked his pulse once more. His heart rate was faint but not fleeting. I was upset that he wasn't dead. Yet, I was happy that he wasn't dead. I took this opportunity to inflict pain upon him. I took out all of my anger on his limp body. He was fully at mercy and wasn't aware of it. I whooped him belts, a metal pole, a pan. I kicked him in various parts of his body. I got revenge.

I needed help getting him to the bed, so I asked my neighbor Ms. Rose to help me. Ms. Rose was an older yet able bodied woman who knew what I was going through. I only needed to ask her to help me get him to bed and she did not hesitate. Once she entered my place and peeped out the scene, she only asked me one question. "Girl, you finally got him! Now what did you do to him?" I started to tell her but she stopped me. "Aht Aht I don't wanna know honey. I'm just glad you got his black ass. Now, I betchu he leaves you alone." I smiled as we lugged his black ass to my bed and tucked him in nicely.

The next morning, the kids and I were up bright and early. The weekend was here and I had a newfound confidence. As me and kids sat watching cartoons, I could hear him waking up. I keep on as normal. He met us in the living room. "Good morning, I see you're finally up." I said.

"What time is it? He asked.

"A little after noon. I made the tuna fish and I think it's some more tea in there."

"PRINCESS! What did do you to me for real? I was up and the next second I was out!"

"Why whatever do you mean? I didn't do anything to you."

"Where my keys at? I gotta go man."

"Your keys are over by the front door. Don't forget your hat. It's in my room on the dresser."

He walks into my room to get his hat and follow him.

"Listen, don't come back to my house no damn more. I don't want to see you nowhere near me. If you wanna see Ishaka, I will make arrangements through my momma. Me and you have nothing else to say to one another!"

"Man, you tripping." He says.

"Yeah, I'm tripping. I've been plotting for months to kill your black ass. Last night, I put Visine in the tea and hoped to take you outta here."

"Yo' ass is crazy! You really want me dead? You tried to kill me with Visine? How in the hell... man you are crazy!"

"Just get out of my house! I mean it don't bother me or next time you will die!"

He left my house that day and I didn't see him for months. He did stop by my mom's house from time to time visiting with Ishaka. I didn't mind that. As long as he didn't bother me; I was well. Life for me and my children became less stressful. I would work as a waitress at then popular commercial seafood restaurant. My pay at the time was $4.75 an hour plus tips earned from customers. I got by okay but it was quite tough being single raising two small children. I'd decided to take a second job which caused me to rely on my parents for additional support. My parents never complained although now looking back; assisting me with my children really cramped their style.

One evening after working both jobs, I went by my parent's house to pick up the kids but they were asleep. My mom didn't want me to wake them and insisted that I leave them to stay overnight. I did as she commanded. The drive home was long on my weary body and tired mind. I couldn't wait to get home. Just as I'd pulled into the parking lot located at the end of a very dark street; I saw a shadow of person. It startled me but I paid that feeling no mind as the neighborhood was quite sketchy to say the least. I gathered my things and existed the vehicle to walk down a dimmed lit sidewalk towards my apartment. That shadowy figure appeared before me holding the trigger of a 9mm Glock 19. It was his black ass back again and with a vengeance. He just couldn't leave me alone. Well, after our last encounter I'm sure he was sore about it.

I stood there tired and frozen. That black ass dude spewed a large amount of threats and unnecessary bombast gung-ho turn of phrases. I stood still… until I couldn't anymore. "Well, nigga if you gon' kill me just do it already. I'm tired anyway. You scary ass bitch, pull the trigger!" Those are the words that I spoke to him. Believe it or not, his black self actually pulled the darn trigger… but it didn't go off!!!! Look at God! I knew it was God covering me that night because his gun was fully loaded and the look in his eyes glazed over with unresolved hatred. He swiftly walked away after the failed gunshot. I didn't look for him; I just told God thank you and went into my house for the remainder of the night. I actually slept quite well.

Since my son's father had decided to resurface in such a horrific manner, I decided to move. This caused for me to break my lease which in turn resulted into an eviction. I didn't bother to call the police as in the past they were no help at all. I didn't tell my family because I really felt like I could resolve this on my own. If I move to a new residence and limit contact with him, then he wouldn't find me… so I thought. I didn't take much with us as to alleviate moving expenses. This would give me the opportunity to redecorate sort of starting over in the same city but a different address. Things were alot different back then as we didn't have internet access as worldwide as we do now.

I told my Section 8 housing counselor about the situation that transpired and she did not hesitate in issuing me a new housing choice voucher. The thing was the Federal Housing Authority of Jacksonville had awarded me a voucher towards renting a new place for myself and children. I would be able to find a rental at the allocated amount according to the Federal Low-Income Household guidelines for my city. This voucher program would be a game changer for my household; I just didn't know it at the time. They say God always has a plan for us; most times were can't see it due to so many of life circumstances. These were my life and my circumstances that kept bound and blind of God's plan for my life.

The Housing Choice Voucher Program allows low-income families the opportunity to rent safe, decent and sanitary privately owned dwelling units. Subsidy payments are made by the Jacksonville Housing Authority to the owners on behalf of the family rather than directly to the family. The subsidy my cover the full amount of rent or depending on the household income a portion of the rent is covered by the voucher and the remaining rental balance would the family's responsibility. The program was created by the Housing and Community Development Act of 1974 and is funded by the United States Department of Housing and Urban Development (HUD).

For an under-educated twenty-something black single mother with a criminal record, the Housing Choice Voucher Program was a life saver for me. It gave me the leverage needed to provide a home for my children and still afford a hood-rich lifestyle. I was on the program for ten years before the spirit of excellence that lived within me woke up.

I'd found a quaint little house in West Jax; three bedrooms with two full bathrooms. The house sat on a nice piece of land with green grass, a pecan tree and the cutest fig tree. It was something about that fig tree gave me a sense of a feeling like I was on my way. On my way where; I had no idea. The first thing that I'd done was decorate my kids' rooms; Penny Proud was theme for my daughter's room and Spider Man for my son. My bedroom was the last thing to decorate as I needed to ensure the living room area was inviting for my children and welcoming for guests. I adorned my kitchen with a nice dining room table and decorated the area in a then modern chic southern country theme. It was our home.

Alaisja has always been a scholar and enjoyed her reading space. I didn't buy toys often as I felt that some toys were frivolous entertainment for children and distractions for the parent. We spent time mastering homework assignments and discussing geography, history, and whatever else was on their brilliant little minds. Ishaka often had trouble sleeping at night which I figured were night terrors. I would allow to fall asleep in my bed watching Spaghetti Westerns and Martial Arts movies. Kill Bill was a particular favorite of mine for obvious reasons.

By now, I'd landed a medical coding position with Optimal Billing Solutions. The pay was decent enough for me to not have to work a second job. This afforded me more time with my children as well as a little night life. The little night life was not wasted at all as me and Zhane stayed in the most popular clubs in the city. Fun don't owe me a thing, ya hear me!

Just as things started to go well for myself and kids; I hear car pulling into my driveway on good Saturday afternoon. I pull back the kitchen curtains and saw a car that I didn't recognize. I dried my hands on a towel to dispel of the dishwater dripping from them. I hurried to my front door and my heart dropped to my feet as I opened the door. It was him hanging from the passenger side of his baby mommas's car. "I wanna see my boy!" he yells. I was flabbergasted. The audacity of him to pull up to my house with *her* and their daughter in the back seat of the car. The nerve! I firmly yet politely asked him to leave my house. He steps out of the car to approach me as I stood on the porch. I walked towards him and met him at the third step; at which time I pulled a knife from my pocket and placed it in at his abdomen with force; "Nigga leave my damn house before I gut you where you stand!" Now, why would I say that? I guess it was from all of the westerns I'd been watching. Hmmm; it worked. He walked away laughing and they drove off.

I knew he would be back. How did he find me? No one outside of family, Zhane and Kirk knew where I lived. Ugh, he irks my last good nerve. I wasn't prepared to move again. Dang, we'd just moved there. The children were in school and thriving. The overall neighborhood left a lot to be desired; yet it was home. Finally! The next few weeks after his miraculous appearance, I would come home after working, picking up the kids etc. and find notes on my door, dead animals; it was wild. I had to think quickly. I needed a solution which would allow us to stay in our home and continue our normal lives.

The last straw was when the black ass dude pulled his truck behind my house and sat there throughout the night. He did this act for four nights too many. That prompted me to execute my plan. I called an old friend, Dante. Dante was from Miami, real handsome with "good hair." He wasn't much for conversation but he was surely easy on the eyes and he was beast in the streets. I romanced Dante and convinced him to move in with me. Dante became our household protector and my flunky. Dante was such a gentleman and a very kind man to my children. I totally mistreated him; all because my heart belonged to another. I never told Kirk about the abuse from the black ass dude; it was too embarrassing. I didn't want Kirk to see me like that…

Dante provided for us until I found out that he had a wife. This man lived with us for seven months and never told me that he had a wife and a kid. I also found out that he had a cocaine problem. Like, what the hell? Knowing all of this, I decided to kick him to the curb; but not after payday. Dante made sure that I received his paychecks every Friday. I would allow him to cash his pay check and give him seventy-five dollars; I kept the rest. He didn't have a problem with it.

Dante's payday rolled around and I was there to pick him up from work. After he entered the car; he reached into his pocket, pulled out the check and handed it to me. As he was doing all of that, he was telling how he'd just been fired from his job. I abruptly pulled the car over and told him to get out. You don't have a job. You're married with a kid… I have had no more use for him. I gave him back his check and pulled off leaving Dante on the side of Arlington

Expressway. My children were in the car; they witnessed this. I didn't care at the time but later this act came back to haunt me when my son got older!

I cleared Dante's things from our house by sitting all he had on the curb to awake trash pick-up. Thinking back, that was so uncool of me. I decided to move again as Dante wasn't there anymore to protect us. I'd sent my kids to my mother's house as I sorted my life out. I told my landlord that there was mice problem and I couldn't live in that house anymore. I was allowed to break yet another lease. I got a new voucher and found new house in Arlington which was a step up from where we were.

I'd quit my job because I didn't know how much the black ass dude had found out about me. I couldn't take any chances. Just before moving into the house in Arlington, I found out that I was pregnant. The thought of having three children killed every dream I'd had of living a better life. All things now centered on me being the best mom and disciplinarian I could be. My life was over but my children would have a solid moral and educational upbringing. The house was big enough for each of us to enjoy own rooms. The front and backyard areas were pleasing to the eye. The neighbors were quite homeowners. This house was perfect!

Without employment income my voucher covered all of my rent and left a stipend for my electric bill. That wasn't enough. Even though I was in denial of my pregnancy for the first 6 months; however, I was aware that my financial situation needed a boost. So, I decided to open a daycare. This decision would afford me the opportunity to be home with my children and solidify a viable income that would, in turn, give me a little financial freedom.

My in-home daycare started with two infants. Their care was free as the mothers were in a financial situation that triggered a memory and prompted compassion. That came to be one of the best decision I'd made at the time because that one act of kindness brought me tons of business. I had to refuse many children because I didn't have staff. I did; however, enroll three toddlers. Due to influx of new business, I made the decision turn my garage into a classroom. This gave me the chance to teach the toddlers as well as provide an amazing study space for my children. Things were looking up.

The children enrolled at my daycare were learning French, Math and Arithmetic. I enjoyed utilizing my High School foreign language expertise. I hadn't spoken French since I was in 10th grade but I remembered the basics. I checked out books that I used to teach the children as well as hone my personal skills. My home had become a place of learning and that I thoroughly appreciated.

The kids and I were in full swing of things from dancing, learning to nap time and lunch. I was in the kitchen cleaning up our dishes and all of sudden I heard the most detrimental sound I could ever hear… gun shots! There were so many gun shots within seconds. I dashed my pregnant body to the floor. I somehow ran and crawled at the time towards the living room where the children were sitting. The children; oh my God, the children were crying at the top of their lungs. I gathered all of them underneath me as the mayhem continued. I started to pray asking God to protect the children. I begged God to not allow harm to the children. And just like the attack on my home ceased.

I waited a moment until I heard my daughter Alaisja say, "Ma, we can get up now." I turned to look at her; the look on her face was calm but angry. "Ma, it was HIM!" How did she know it was HIM? I consoled all of the children and checked each of them from to toe; no one was harmed. I called the police and then made contact with each parent, advising them of the situation. Those parents were there in what appeared to be seconds. No one was angry with me; I was completely thankful for that. Though, I wouldn't blame them if they were. It was refreshing to hear their words of comfort for me and their concerns for my children. To be honest, I didn't know what to do. I was angry, mad, pissed, scared, nervous… all shook up!

The cops arrived just as the last parent was leaving with their children. I stepped outside to welcome the officers just to be paused by the one in charge. "Wait right there, ma'am," the officer commanded. I stopped in my tracks as he'd asked. I couldn't wait to spill my guts. I waited anxiously for the officers to acknowledge me. Just then, one of the cop cars pulled off. I was a little puzzled as to why that cop pulled off from the scene. Alaisja came out of the front door and stood next to me. She grabbed my hand in a manner that provided a level of comfort I didn't realize was needed.

The officer in charge made his way to me. He was a stocky white guy with tattoos that covered both arms and his neck. I remembered him. He was the same officer that I'd call a few years back to report the initial abuse. The words that he spoke to me back then came rushing into my mind like a flood; "You're just going to take him." I never took him back. I had been running and hiding from this guy for so long. I snapped myself back into the present to hear the officer say, "Now, ma'am tell me what happened." I told the guy everything from start to finish. Alaisja chimed in and said, "It was my brother's dad." The officer sarcastically asked her, "How do you it was him?" Alaisja replied, "Because I saw him. When my mom was getting the other kids, I was in my room and I peeked out the window and I saw him." My heart skipped several beats. My daughter could have been hit by one the bullets. I reached for her and pulled her into my embrace.

"Ma'am, I have more questions," the officer said. "Yes, sir," was my response. "Now, how many kids are in the house now?" I told him. "How many were in the house at the time of the incident?" I told him. His next statements rocked my world. "Well ma'am, all I can do is take a statement. It appears to me that everyone is fine. He's not here so I cannot do anything further." What the hell? I couldn't believe what I was hearing. "To be honest, I cannot just take the word of kid. I have no way of knowing if you coached her to say those things." It felt like I was being abused all over again. He did issue a trespassing citation against my son's dad. He told me that I could pick the report in a week from the police station. He also gave me a book that included a few numbers that I could call for help. Hell, isn't that what 9-1-1 is for?

CHAPTER 19

Life or Death

At this point, it was my life or his. I was sick of being sick and tired. It was time for me to take action. Everybody around me thought it is was game. No one took any of these actions seriously. It was like wanting to be rescued from a burning building but no one knew you were in there and no one could hear you crying. This was my life and I couldn't sit back to wait for someone to rescue me. I had to rescue myself. I'd sent my children to my mom's house for a few days to give me some time to come up with a plan. I'm just going to kill him; that's it.

After leaving my mom's house, I went back home and started cleaning my place. I had the windows replaced and reinforced the locks on every door. I loaded my gun and sat in the middle of my living room with tears flowing nonstop. I held my pregnant stomach and realized that I had to think about the lives of my children. If I were to kill that man, my kids would be motherless and I would be having my baby in jail. That would be just too ghetto than what was already ghetto. Think Princess… no Pray Princess.

I knew all of the mistakes that I'd made in the past. I knew all of the stuff that happened to me as a child. I carried so much shame, pain, resentment, anger, frustration and dismay. All of those feelings controlled my entire being. I was so tired of carrying everything. Having to fight a fight that was fixed and set against me to lose. A well-dressed mess of woman. A mediocre mother. A half ass citizen. A total wreck drowning in the abyss of life. Maybe if I removed myself from existence perhaps it would rewire the universe in favor of my children. But, I cannot kill myself after all I am carrying a baby. What am I going to do?

I sat there for hours with hollowed thoughts. Something overwhelmed me, prompting me to pray. I started by confessing all of my deepest feelings to God. "Lord God, I am in such pain. I am so confused. Everything is so messed up. Why is this happening to me? Why would let my life be like this? I know I am not perfect. I know that I haven't been a good person; but God I am trying. Please help me and my children. Lord God, if you help me through this, I promise I will help somebody else that's going through what I am going through now. I promise if you help, I will do my best to be whomever you'd have me to be. Lord, I need you."

I fell asleep on that floor and didn't even realize it until the next morning. I found the book that the officer had given me and called the hotline number listed. I hung up. How was I going to tell someone all of my tea without them judging me? I called downtown to the police station to inquire about the trespassing citation and the report the officer told me to check on in a week. A woman answered the phone and told her why I was calling. She transferred me to someone else; who then told me that I would need to go to court to fully have the trespassing citation enforced. I followed her instructions and a court date was set for a week from that day.

I called my friend Zhane and told her what happened. She came over to check on me. We sat and talked about different the many different things that were going on in our lives. I couldn't believe that she'd gotten married and never told me. I mean, we literally talked every day. She told me about their fights and I mean him beating the crap out her in front of her children. Have mercy, what did we ever do to deserve this? Zhane was a hard worker. A woman who was not only beautiful but someone you could count on. I asked if she was going to leave her husband. Zhane told me and that she loved him. I guess that was difference between the two of us, I didn't love that guy. We said our good-byes. For some reason, I didn't tell Zhane about my plans and knowing what I know now; I'm glad I didn't.

My court date came and I was Johnny on the spot. I didn't think his black ass would show up; but he did. The judge called our case and it was time for me stand up for myself.

Judge: "Hi, Mr. Black Ass Dude."

Him: "Good Morning, Your Honor. You don't remember me?"

Judge: "I remember you, sir."

Him: "It was two years ago when I stood before you about those allegations"

Judge: "Yes, I remember."

I stood there confused about their back and forth. But from the look on the judge's face it may work in my favor.

Judge: "Ms. Booker, I've looked over the police report and I must say that I am shocked. Could you tell me in your own words why we are here this morning?

Me: Through waited breaths I spoke, "Yes ma'am. I am just tired he keeps finding me and my children no matter where I move to. He has pulled a gun on and pulled the trigger. He has taken my son away from me and called me daily taunt me. He has broken into my home and threatened me. He won't stop and now he has shot up my house. I am not safe. My children are not safe."

Judge: "Give Ms. Booker a tissue." The judge beckoned the bailiff.

The bailiff gave me the tissue with tears in his eyes he returned to his post.

Judge: "Ms. Booker, I am going to appoint you a Victim's Advocate. Please stand next to Ms. Booker for the duration. Now, Ms. Booker what do you want?

Me: "I want him to leave us alone. Leave me alone. The officer said that there wasn't anything that he could do to help me. So, I don't know."

Him: "She's lying Your Honor. I haven't done any of that."

Judge: "Sir, I remember you. I remember what you stood before about two years. Please be silent until I ask you a question."

His black ass stood there in awe but silent.

Judge: "Ms. Booker; May I call you Princess?"

Me: "Yes ma'am." I said through the sniffles.

Judge: "How many children do you have?"

Me: "I have two and the one I'm carrying."

Judge: "How many are by Him?"

Me: "My son; just one."

Judge: "Okay, here's what I'm going to do. Ms. Booker, I am granting you an injunction. He will not be able to come near you or your children for the next three years. I am ordering you and your children into the local Domestic Violence Shelter immediately."

Me: "Will I have time to get my children and some of our things? My son has severe asthma and a skin condition."

Judge: "Yes, you have 24 hours to report to the shelter or I am opening up a Child Protective case. You either comply or you will lose your children."

Me: "Yes ma'am. I will comply. Thank you so much! Thank you!"

Judge: "Black Ass Dude did you understand my ruling?"

Him: "Yes ma'am, but I didn't get a chance to say anything."

Judge: "Well since you understood my ruling for your sake I hope you abide by it. If I see you before me again, I will not give you the benefit of the doubt!"

~Case closed

Just as the judge mandated, I packed as much of our things as possible and headed to the shelter. I had my mom and grandmother take us as I didn't know if I could bring my car. I'd never been in a shelter before. My mom was totally against this. She accused me of over reacting. Of course she would, in her mind I was a *Drama Queen*. I didn't listen to her, I had to do what was best for myself and children. My granny didn't say a word. I assumed she was disappointment in me just as my mom. The ride seemed so long even though it took only fifteen minutes for us to get there. As my children and I were existing their van, my granny grabbed my hand and squeezed it tightly yet affectionately. I needed that reassurance.

The kids and I made our way to the front door of the shelter. I grabbed the door handled and took a deep breath before opening. Before we entered, I told me my kids that things were going to better for us. I asked them to trust me and I apologized to them. I glanced up at the sky and told God thank you. We entered the building and we didn't look back.

Upon checking into the shelter, we were acknowledge by three women. Before we were allowed to settle in, we were interviewed. I guess the judge's orders came as a shock to them and wanted to make sure all things said in the order were real. The three excused themselves from the tiny room. Only one came back and offered to gives a tour of the facility. I was a bit taken back by the living conditions along with the rules. However, it was refreshing to have a place where the kids and I were safe. "You all will be staying on the third floor. Now, there's only two other families up there. You will have a shared kitchen and living space but the sleeping quarters are separate. No one is allowed on third floor your family and theirs. You will not be able to leave the facility at any point. In the next two days, you will be assign a counselor to assess your situation and to help you navigate through all of this. The kids will start school once receive their records from the school board. I know you're pregnant, you will receive prenatal care once we figure out how to get you to and from the facility safely. Do you have any questions?" I didn't have any questions at the time. The woman unlocked the door to our room and opened it... it was huge. Each of us a bed of our own. There was a full bathroom; we didn't have to share with anyone. It was perfect for us.

The woman left us to settle in. My children stood in the middle of the room looking over the space. It wasn't what they were used to,

I could see their dismay. I called them towards me and I placed my arms around them. I told them that this situation would only be temporary and to trust me. My son looked up at me and asked, "Momma are we here because of my daddy?" I wanted to cry but I held back the tears. I didn't lie to him. "Momma, why did he shoot at us?" Can you imagine your child asking you why his dad shot at him? "Lord, son he wasn't shooting at ya'll. He was shooting at me." That's what I told him which was actually the truth. His dad loved him but hated me. I don't even think he hated me; I believed he was just delusional about our relationship status. Sometimes the worst thing you could say to a person is *I don't want to be with you anymore.*

I held them kids so tight and the hugged me. We needed that. Alaisja asked me about school, of course. Ishaka got his wrestling men out his bookbag. I told Alaisja that they would be back in school soon and to continue her reading to ensure she doesn't get behind. My mom had packed us some food for evening. We sat together and ate. I put my children to bed and sat in silence for a moment. I couldn't hold back the tears any more. I was afraid honestly I didn't know what was in store for us. What was I going to do? My heart was heavy in pain and despair. I called upon the only help that I knew; Jesus. As a kid, I would attend church and hear the pastor and mothers talk about how the name of Jesus was more powerful that anything in this world. Some part of me believed and another part of me didn't feel worthy enough. But maybe my kids; they were innocent.

I cried out in whispers asking God to give me strength. I need to be strong through all of this. I asked God to give me knowledge to carry my family. I believed that God would order my steps and set me on path that would enrich our lives. I had to believe; there was no other way. Before I laid down to sleep; I ended my prayer by saying, *In the name of Jesus.*

The next morning we got up and prayed together. I'd advised my children to not interact with anyone because we didn't know them.

They listened. When we existed our room, the other families were up and about. They introduced themselves and children to me and mine. I will say this, my time in the shelter was a very pivotal moment in our lives. We made friendships that lasted a life time. I fell in love with all of the children, we even celebrated birthdays and milestones.

I'd gotten permission for my mom to bring my computer up to the shelter. I couldn't spend time with her; I only thanked her and received my property. I needed my computer as I was taking online classes towards my A.S. in Human Resources. In the midst of all the chaos in my life, I knew it was necessary for me to get an education if I was going to change my circumstances. I'd kept this a secret with the exception of my Alaisja. My mom not only brought my computer but she also brought me my internet modem from Clear. I hooked my computer up in our room and I do my assignments at night while the children slept.

We were in the shelter for longer than anticipated. I went into labor. My children had to leave the shelter so my mom picked them up. I was rushed to the hospital. However, just before leaving; I was stopped by the Director of the place. She told me not to worry; our room would be waiting for us. That gave me peace of mind. I can never repay her for that. Oh brother! I was in labor again!

This time I was all alone. It felt strange but I was okay with it. There was a kind EMT that asked me, "Are you going to be alone?" I nodded my head forward and lowered it at the same time. Do you know, that guy stayed with me the entire time? I never knew his name; he never gave it. But he stayed until my baby girl entered the world. I didn't know what to name her. I thought about Natalya or Natalia which means Christmas Day. I wasn't completely sold on it so I held off as long as I could. I just knew she was gorgeous.

A knock at the door gathered my attention, in walks Dante. Now who told him that I was in labor? It had to be my mom. He came in there with blue balloons and a blue bear. I didn't want him there. I let him see our daughter. Tears welled in his eyes and I could all the love he had for her. He asked me her name and I told him Natalya. He loved it; but I didn't. I gave him such a hard time. I totally regret that because I didn't allow him in her life for years after this moment. He looked over to me just as he was leaving; "Thank you, Princess for my daughter. I love her and I love you." He left the room. I was angry at him for saying that he loved us.

A nurse with a familiar face walked into our room, "Hey Princess! I came to see the baby." She walks over to my bed and gave me hug. I smiled with reciprocity. She went over to my baby girl laying in her basinet, "Princess, can I hold her?" I told her yes. She gently picked up the baby, "Princess, what's her name?" I told her about the name Natalya; she liked it. Just as she was putting the baby down the familiar nurse said, "What about Azariah?" That name rung loudly in my ears. "It means Yah has helped. It's in The Bible in 2 Chronicles," she said. Wow, how beautiful is that? Azariah it is; but I changed the spelling a bit.

I called the shelter and spoke with the Director, "...everything was successful." We went over ways to keep us safe until we returned to the shelter. I would stay with my parents until after my six week check-up. This gave me time to connect with my family and enjoy my time with them. Being there gave me a sense of home but somehow I knew if I stayed, my life would never get any better. I would continue the same cycle of poverty, violence and piss poor parenting. If I stayed, it would be settling. I was tired of simply existing.

Azariah's six week check-up went well. My wellness check-up was good but the doctor told me that my stress assessment reported that I wasn't managing things so well. The doctor informed me of the risks and gave me a few suggestions to help manage my stress. He didn't know half of things that were going on in my life. I accepted his terms and walked out of that office more determined to change myself; my life. It was time that to become another person. A new mask was created.

Upon returning to my parent's house, I immediately called the shelter. I needed to make sure our room was still available and when would be the best time for us to return. The advocate that answered the phone denied me access and said that I'd given up my space. This meant that I would need to be on a waiting list. I was not satisfied with her answer as I recalled the conversation between myself and the Director. After the advocate paused, I asked to speak with the Director. She initially tried to give me the run around but I insisted. I was placed on a long hold until the advocate returned and annoyingly asked, "You still there?" I responded, ""Yes, I'm still here. I really need to speak with the Director as my situation is a little different from most." "Just hold on then!" That is what the advocate said to me. I did as she insisted. The next voice I heard was that of the Director.

"Ms. Booker, I am so sorry for that. She was not aware of your situation." I was pleased with the Director's message. She told me that we could return to the shelter any time before 4pm. I thanked her and the call ended. I checked the time; it was a quarter past 2pm. I rushed to pack of our things and told the kids to get ready to leave. They were not happy about it; their disappointment showed upon their faces. It broke my heart but we had to leave.

I walked into my mother's room to give her the news. She was not happy either. She insisted that we stay. She tried to convince me that I was making a mountain out of a molehill. I heard her heart through her words; but I needed to do what I felt was best for myself and children. My mom refused to take us back to the shelter. I cried and begged her; she would not move. My grandmother had heard our conversation and walked into my mom's bedroom, "Cynt, get up and take 'em." My mom didn't dare to challenge my granny. Through tears and snot, I turned and looked upon my granny. Her face was stern but her eyes beamed with love and understanding. I found a strength in that moment to go forward with my decision.

The kids and I return to the shelter that afternoon five minutes before 4pm. We'd beaten the cut-off. The Director was still there when we arrived. She told me to take the children upstairs to get them settled and to return downstairs. I did as I was asked; I'd settled the kids and returned downstairs holding my newborn baby girl. The Director met me where I stood and admired my baby. She asked me to follow her into my office. Once we were in her office she went over my new family plan of action. They would relocate me and children at my discretion. This meant that they would cover all of the moving expense and even pay my rent for two months. They would ensure that the restraining order would be extended to where ever I would decide to move.

That was the best news ever! But… where would we go from here? Nowhere that I've been seemed appropriate for the life I was starting to envision. I decided to try Atlantic Beach, FL. It was still in Jacksonville. The neighborhood was familiar as I grew up there. The schools were top tier. But, it was still in Jacksonville! I went to the Director and told her of my decision. I'd found a beautiful house available for rent. They would accept my housing voucher and all. The assigned staff had begun preparing my transition paperwork. I had to meet with an exit counselor to go over my stay at the shelter and to discuss how I would go about living.

The kids were in school and daycare within the shelter. I received a page over the intercom to come meet with the exit counselor. I was eager to meet with her as I'd felt good about my choices. The exit counselor was an older Native American woman. Her style of dress was similar to Dorothy from the Golden Girls sitcom. She wore a pleasant smile which was inviting. I entered her office and extended my hand for a shake. She hugged me instead. That was needed.

After such a delightful greeting, we sat down to chat. The conversation didn't go as expected. The exit counselor started by introducing herself beyond just her name. She shared her story with me. She survived domestic violence from a spouse. She actually had to leave her kids behind just to rescue herself. She later returned and obtain full custody of children which also granted her spousal support. She told me something that didn't know about the other counselors at the shelter; they were are survivors! Many of them were volunteers. I couldn't believe that. However, it explained a lot. Knowing that definitely changed my perception of those women. For some, I admired. Others, it made me wonder why they would treat the residents the way they did.

The exist counselor held my file in hand. She commended me on my bravery to seek help and attending college. However, she pointed out that the weaknesses of plan. Finding a home in the same city where my attacker resided wasn't wise. It left me vulnerable. My rebuttal was that I would have family support. Her response shook my soul; you family is also a part of the problem. When she said that, I broke down in tears. It was true. The exit counselor also stated that I needed psychological therapy. She suggested this due to the childhood traumas that I'd experienced and due to my current situation.

Psychological therapy? Did that mean I was crazy? In my Black American family, the thought of seeking therapy was ambivalent. There were mixed feelings and/or contradictive ideas regarding the subject. Dealing with sexual assault, child abuse, child neglect and the like were whispered conversations that simply became the norm. The best was to deal with those things were to not deal with them. Take it to God in prayer and leave it there. Nonetheless, it was helping me. I needed to understand the why in these situations. Why was abused and neglected? Why was I finding myself in relationships that hurt me? Why? The exit counselor was right. Our conversation left me with more questions than answers.

I left her office with a heavy heart. The ball was in motion for my transition but I wasn't ready to leave just yet. I needed to tell the Director but how? I didn't want to let her down. I didn't want her to think I wasn't serious about my goals. I had to tell her. I figured that I would send her an email. Yeah, an email would be the best way to tell. I went up to my room and logged into my computer. *Dear Ms. Director...*

I'd decided not to move into the house in Atlantic Beach. I needed to make a decision quickly as the assistance program gave me a deadline. After the kids returned back to my care for the afternoon, I prepared dinner and put the baby down for a nap. Alaisja and Ishaka worked on their homework. I'd decided to talk to the other mother's on my floor. I wanted know their opinions. Talking to them didn't give me any answers; just more questions. My mind was a maze of thoughts and cluster of unanswered questions. Well, since I couldn't focus on that let me log into my online classes. I might as well get some classwork assignments done; I was already behind from going out on maternity leave.

CHAPTER 20

To be or Not to be

Putting the kids down for the night seemed to be more of a chore than usual. Ishaka's asthma flared up and needed to be tended to. Azariah refused to go to sleep and cried something fierce. Alaisja was frustrated as she was genuinely tire and wanted to sleep. My emotions were running high as I still needed to make decisions that were critical for our livelihood. I was able to finally pull myself together and get the kids down for the night. Alaisja stepped in to help me with Ishaka which allowed me to care for Azariah. The room was finally quiet but I couldn't sleep.

Sitting at the edge of my bed, a calm resolve overwhelmed me. Pray! I needed to hear from God. I asked God to hear my heart. I needed to know what He would have me to do. I laid out all that was presented to me by the Director, the exit counselor and my mom. I told God my plans and expressed my desires. As sat in the dark quiet room, I had an urge to write down my thoughts and feelings, listing the pros and cons of my choices that lay before me. I didn't hear anything. I grew restless. I checked on the children ensuring they were sound in their sleep.

I left the room and walked the halls of the shelter. Something drew me to the computer room. I walked into the computer, all of the lights were off. It was past access hours so I left the lights off as I sat down at the second computer from the front door. I made sure the volume off to cloak my mission. I sat there and heard a voice say search Rhode Island. Now the voice wasn't a sound from physical person. It was a sound without a known physical source; benevolence.

I did as the voice instructed and typed Rhode Island into the search bar. I pressed Enter on the keyboard. Voila! Just like that everything about the state of Rhode Island appeared on the screen. I sat there combing through the information, just as I heard the voice instruct me to look up domestic violence shelters in Providence. I did as instructed; but it wasn't much information on there. I printed out the data that was available and made a plan to call each place the next day. Just as I was about to end my search, I felt a gentle hand on my left shoulder. I looked around the computer room; there was no one there but me. Startled a bit but I felt assured. I didn't move. I waited for instructions from the voice. Just then, I saw on the screen the name of shelter in Providence, Rhode Island with telephone line opened 24hours. I called.

The phone rang three times before a pleasant feminine voice spoke, "Hello." My response was, "Hello and hi. My name is Princess Booker. I am currently living in a shelter in Jacksonville, Florida with my three children...." I laid out my entire situation in one breath. The woman on the other end simply replied, "If you can get here we will help you." Okay, that was the plan. I was going to a shelter in Providence, Rhode Island. I went back to my room to find my children still sound asleep. I was happy and enthusiastic about my new plan. I laid down for bed and told God thank you. I slept well.

The next morning, I took the children to daycare and school inside the shelter. I went to the counseling center and added my name to the list as I needed to communicate this plan to the Director and the exit counselor. I kept my move hidden from everyone else. I heard my name over the intercom; I didn't waste time getting downstairs. It was my time to inform them of my plan. I entered the counseling office and was told that everyone was waiting on me in the Director's office. Now, who the heck was everyone?

I got to the Director's office and knocked gingerly. I entered the room upon being welcomed and saw five women sitting them looking at me. The Director introduced me to everyone and offered me a seat. "Now, Ms. Booker, tell us what you've decided. We are all here to help," said the Director. I told them of my plan to relocate to Providence, Rhode Island. They asked me where we would be staying.

I told them about the shelter. The looks on their faces showed their confusion and concern. "Ms. Booker, may I ask why Rhode Island, a woman asked. I told her that God told me to go there. They were not accepting of my answer. I explained to the ladies what happened to me in the computer room the evening that I'd heard the voice and felt the touch. All of them but one looked at me as if I'd lost my mind. The one gave me her words of wisdom and approval, "Ms. Booker, this is all new to us. Your entire file leaves us in dismay. If God gave you directions, you must follow them." I appreciated her in that moment.

The Director told me that they could only give me $1500 to assist with my relocation. I had to sign off any further assistance needed from them. They gave three days to solidify my plans and from there I would excused from the program. I was shocked yet I conceded. I walked away with the understanding that I was on my own. The $1500 check came and I was escorted to my bank to cash it. I deposited a check into my account. Upon my arrival back to the office, I logged into my computer to check out transportation options. I couldn't travel by bus as it would take too long. I couldn't travel by train as that would be unbearable for me and the children. I checked flights on Expedia and found our one-way tickets to Providence, Rhode Island. The cost of the tickets were a little over twelve hundred dollars.

The night before we left for our new home in strange place, I sat the children down just before bed and explained to them what was going on. I described it as an adventure similar to Gulliver's travels. They found it funny and Alaisja labeled us as nomads. A family without a fixed home who regularly moved to and from. It was funny at the time but later, I realized that it wasn't funny. In turn, it was a tad disturbing. My children and I moved from place to place due to financial and socio-economic crisis tied together with violence. While moving around so much gave us temporary stability and safety, it was quite difficult for them to develop friendships and such. That was not the plan; honestly somewhere along the journey the plan became distorted. I just rolled with whatever life was sending my way. Until I heard the voice.

I was afraid, agitated, apprehensive, concerned, hesitant, excited as well as optimistic. As the children slept, I prayed. I'd asked God to stop my plans if I moving in error. I told God all of my feelings and emotions. I shed even more tears; a mixture of happy and sad. Before I knew it the sun was coming up. This was the day for us to embark on our new journey. I had no clue what to expect as I'd only read about Rhode Island in history books. I knew no one. I didn't know how things were going work out. I didn't know who I would encounter. I had not decided on what I wanted to accomplish. I only knew that I would trust God. I would be brave in the midst of my fears. I knew that I had all that I needed; me, myself, God and my children.

My children caught a cab to Jacksonville Airport. That cost me approximately twenty dollars out of the money given to me. Each of us had only a back pack a piece which we all carried. I carried Azariah's baby bag and a small bag with her clothes. Aside from that we each only had the clothes and shoes on our backs. We had snacks for the trip which I'd obtain from the food pantry at the shelter. After checking in and arriving at the departure gate, it took less than an hour for them call all passengers. It was time us to go.

We boarded the plane and I didn't know about assigned seating. I just knew Ishaka and Alaisja would sit together near me and Azariah. An older white woman became enraged because apparently we'd taken her seat. Her display embarrassed me. I didn't know what to do. I apologized to her and begged her pardon. I tried to explain to her that I just wanted for me and children to sit together. This chaos drew the attention of staff and passengers alike. The older white woman said to me, "I don't know why you're traveling with such small children anyway!" I replied, "No, you don't! You don't know anything about us. I have tried to apologize to you but you just keep yelling at me." I just knew we were about to be kicked off of the plane when I saw the female stewardess walk over to us. But, it quite the opposite. The stewardess told the old woman that they'd found her a seat in first-class. She pointed the old white woman to the direction of another. The stewardess apologized to me and my children and assured us that our current seating was just fine. Some of the passengers even helped me with them during the flight.

    The children really enjoyed the flight. They loved looking out of the window and watching the clouds. Azariah didn't cry not one time. We had no layovers so our flight to Providence landed after two hours and thirty five minutes. It was time for us to exit the plane. I let all of the other passengers exit before I got the kids together. I grabbed each of their little hands and said a prayer for protection. The female stewardess that had stood up for me came over to us and wished us well. She helped us off of the plane and even walked out of the arrival doors.

    I hailed a cab and gave the cabby the address to the shelter. He recognized the address and asked if we had any family. I lied and said yes; I didn't want a stranger to know our plight. However, I think that he knew I was lying. As we rode to our destination, I looked out the window checking out the scenery. It was incompatible to any place I'd seen in my life. We arrived to the shelter.

    Providence; I still needed to digest the fact that we were in Rhode Island. The word *providence* means the protective care of God or of nature as a spiritual power. Providence is the guardianship and care provided by a deity or god. The word provide is a clue to the word's meaning as when a religious being is said to give people providence, it means he/or she is taking care of them-providing for them. In the Bible God's providence means that everything happens for a reason. Be it big or small; good or bad. Ultimately, it is for a good reason; a greater purpose. For in providence God is working out all things according to the counsel of His perfectly good will. I read that in Ephesians 1:11.

Upon our arrival to the shelter in Providence I felt like I was supposed to be there. I was overcome with a feeling of relief. My children and I entered the building and was greeted by a familiar voice. It was the woman who answered my phone call late that night while I was in the computer room. You know the night that I heard the voice. Things were starting to make sense. The woman welcomed us and started to ask me questions while walking towards her desk. I began to remind her that I was the person who'd called from Florida. She was shocked. She couldn't believe that we'd travelled so far and under the circumstances. The kind woman said to me, "Well Ms. Booker, this facility isn't equipped to help you. You have small children." I held back tears and the words seemed heavy in my throat as I said, "We don't have nowhere else to go. We don't anybody here. I've travelled so far away from home…"

The kind woman gently lifted her right hand to stop me from speaking. I paused my words and allowed her to speak. "Ms. Booker, you all can stay here for the night. We will find some place for you and your children to go in the morning. We can't put you with the rest of the population so you all will have stay in the playroom upstairs while we sort this out. Don't worry." I accepted her suggestion it wasn't like we had any other options. She showed us to our sleeping area and asked if were hungry. The kids immediately said yes. She had someone bring us our food, hamburgers without bread and a side of early peas.

The kids ate their food and attempted to play with the toys in the room. I fed Azariah, so she was content. I pulled out my Boost Mobile cellphone to check my account balance. The automated voice stated that my account balance was ten cent. Ten Cent!!! I am in Providence, RI with three children sitting in playroom with no place to go and ten cent in my bank account being told not to worry. Lord have mercy! I had to hold myself together. I could let the children see my upset. I decide to get up and engage them in play. We played and laughed until Alaisja retreated to her book and Ishaka to his fidget spinners. I sat back down on the sofa and picked up Azariah to change her diaper. With my nerves on end I rocked my baby girl and song the theme song to the Golden Girls. Do not ask me why I chose that song; it was simply the first tune that came to mind. Nevertheless, Azariah seemed to enjoy it.

    The day was drawing nigh and in walked the kind woman with mats and blankets for us. She showed us where the restroom was and ensured us that we were safe as no one would be allowed up there. I washed the kids up in the restroom and allowed them to brush their teeth. I finally got them all down for bed. I sat up praying, "Lord God, I know you didn't have me come all the way here for this. I know what you told me. I listened to you. Please help us. I need you." I got grabbed my blanket and placed it over me. I didn't sleep as I needed to watch over my children.

    The morning came fast. The kind woman entered the playroom with good news. "Ms. Booker, we've found you a place to go. We contacted the shelter in Florida and they told us about your situation and we've found the perfect place for you. It is not in Providence. It's in Cranston." Cranston, I thought. I didn't know anything about the geography of Rhode Island. I told the kind woman thank you and expressed my appreciation. She was also relieved as she hadn't been to sleep either. She didn't go home until she was able to come up with a solution for us. I didn't know how we were going get to the shelter in Cranston. "Ma'am, I don't have any more money. I only have…" The kind woman interjected, "Don't worry about it. We are going to take care of it."

I was given a ticket to give to the cab driver that came to pick us up from the shelter in Providence to take us to Cranston. It was the same cabby that had picked us from the airport. He was Egypt. During the ride, the cabby told us all about his childhood growing up in Egypt confirming that Egypt was in Africa. I've read many books so when he started to talk about the Continent I could engage. That communication lessen my fear and took my mind off of the worry of it all. As we drove to Cranston we passed through a few cities such as Narragansett and Pawtucket. Those name stuck out to me as I started to realize that they were Native American names.

The twelve minute ride seemed much longer than it was. We arrived to our destination. It was yellow house with beautiful green grass with a playset that set on side of it. I looked at the cabby to confirm that we were indeed the right place. He nodded his head forward and wished us well. With baby in tow and my other two children at each side me, we approach the house. The front door opened swiftly and a beautiful Hispanic woman greeted us. She showed us around the house, we were the only residents at the time. It was a domestic shelter but it looked more like a home. Full kitchen, living room, a huge upstairs area and cable television. This set-up was much different from the one in Jacksonville.

The beautiful Hispanic woman that greeted us was actually a counselor at the facility. After showing us around she told that I would need to check in with her after I got the children situated. I'd told the kids to sit tight and advised Alaisja to look after her siblings while I go downstairs to meet with the counselor. The beautiful Hispanic woman had an office that sat adjacent to the living room area. I found her and started the intake process. I advised her that I was in school and my classes were online. I wasn't allowed to connect my computer inside the facility but there was a local library just down the street. I needed to enroll the Alaisja and Ishaka into school; she provided with me the local schools information and gave me directions to it. It was in walking distance. As the conversation came to a close I was a given a list of rules which were comprehensive and understandable. I told her that we were hungry. She immediately showed me to the kitchen and advised me that I was able to cook whatever I wanted just clean up behind myself. That was a remarkable difference as the shelter in Jacksonville was very different. The residents were able to cook meals but we had the food was rationed out to us.

I went upstairs to get the children and told them that I was cooking us dinner. Their little eyes lit up. There was a delightful Corner Nook Dining Set that sat in the huge kitchen along with a high chair. I placed Azariah into the high chair and the other two sat at the table. This was beautiful to see. I opened the refrigerator door and saw vast amount of fresh vegetables. I opened the freezer and found more than enough of protein. I opened the cabinets and they were fully stocked. My goodness what was I going to cook? I turned to the children and asked them for suggestions and simultaneously the shouted, "Pancakes!" Pancakes? These kids wanted pancakes. Pancakes it is!

The next day, I found a baby stroller and strapped Azariah in. We out for the day to check out the neighborhood. It was pleasant with a small town feel. It was beautiful, stunningly breathtaking. I had the address for the school memorized so when we happened upon the street, I decided to walk towards its location. We stood outside of the school and told Alaisja and Ishaka that I would be enrolling them there come the morrow. We continued our walk and headed back to the shelter. It was finally a good day!

The next day I enrolled them into school. There was no daycare for Azariah so she stayed with me. After enrolling the children into school, I made my way to the local library and logged into my classes. Azariah sat in her stroller while I worked. She was such a good baby. I did this every day until it was time for us to leave. I had a little free time on my hands before walking to pick the kids up from school. I would take Azariah to the park and sit with her until it was time.

One afternoon while sitting in the park, I heard the voice again. The voice advised me that I need to call the Jacksonville Housing Authority about my voucher. I figured that I would call them the next day but the voice told me that it needed to done immediately. I hurried back to the library as I needed internet access to look the information. The library was closed. I walked down to the shelter and asked one of the counselors to allow me access to their computer. I explained to that I needed to find the telephone number for the Jacksonville Housing Authority. She told me no. She then asked me for the name of the place. I gave it to her. She went into their office and obtained the information for me. I was grateful.

I left the shelter in a hurry as I was running late for pick-up. As I walked down the street towards the school, I called the housing authority in Jacksonville from my cellphone. I finally reached the department I was looking for. Just as I was being connected to my housing counselor, I could see Alaisja and Ishaka heading my way. My housing counselor answered the phone, "Ms. Booker where are you?" I told her that I was in Cranston, Rhode Island and why I was there. "Ms. Booker why didn't you call me? We could have helped you. Listen, follow these instructions." I listened to her instructions as I greeted my children. My housing counselor's instructions advised me to contact the Providence Housing Authority and have someone from there to call her.

The next day, I did as she asked. I called the Providence Housing Authority and told them what my housing counselor in Florida had told me. I was transferred to someone more equipped to assist than the receptionist. I repeated everything that I'd told the receptionist. The woman made me an appointment. She told that I could not miss my appointment or else I would be placed on a waiting list. I talked to the counselors at the shelter and told them everything that was going on. They were a reluctant to believe me and called their supervisor. The supervisor came in the next day and met with me. I told her everything. She approved my leave and paid for my transportation to and from the Providence Housing Authority.

The day of appointment finally came. I arrived on-time with all three of my children. The woman at the place was shocked. "Ms. Booker I didn't think that you were going to come. I've spoken with your housing counselor in Florida and we have a voucher ready for you today." I couldn't believe it. She explained to me how the program worked. I understood as it was the same as Florida. I had thirty days to find a place or my voucher would be expired.

I returned to the shelter and excitingly informed the staff that I'd received a new housing voucher from the Providence Housing Authority. They all were happy for me. I had to come up with a plan of action on finding a place to stay. The beautiful Hispanic woman came to me as I prepared dinner. She told me that I would qualify for welfare from the state. She provided me with a document that contained all of the information needed to apply. I thanked her graciously and continued preparing my meal. The very next day after walking the kids to school, I called the number from the document. I was told that I need to come into their office which was located in Providence. I was told that walk-ins were welcomed from 10am to 2pm Monday thru Thursday. I went back to the shelter and checked in informing them that I needed to be to the welfare office in Providence at the appointed times given. The staff arranged my transport but it was not a cab. I was given money for the bus. The bus; why I'd never! Yeah, right beggars can't be choosers.

The following week, the children and I boarded a bus from Cranston to the City of Providence. Public transportation was very different from the City of Jacksonville. The buses were on-time for one. The other thing was people were allowed to stand while the bus was in motion. Everyone rode the bus, from the seedy to the polished.

It very different indeed. Well pulled into main terminal. After getting off of the bus, the hustle and bustle of people moving in and people moving out was such a sight to see. I held on to my babies for dear life. I saw what I thought was a friendly face and asked her where I could find the welfare office. The woman noticed my southern accent and chuckled. I didn't know what she laughing for but I paid her no never mind as I needed to know how to get to the welfare office. The woman told me that I would need to board another bus and tell the driver where I needed to get off. I took her directions as she stated them.

We arrived at to the welfare office just in time to be seen. I checked in at the front counter and waited to be seen. A frail older white man walked from the foyer, "Booker," he shouted. I didn't make him wait. I made haste in his direction and followed his lead to dimly lit cubicle. I gave him the copies of the documents showing that I resided in the shelter in Cranston. He asked me for proof of mine and the children's identity. I provided him the appropriate verifications. He stepped away for all of three minutes and returned with a card. I was awarded thirteen hundred dollars in cash and the same in food stamps. Florida would never!

I would use this money in correlation with my voucher to find an apartment in North Providence. The place was nice and clean. The neighborhood was clean and quiet. It was near grocery and department stores. The best part about it was that there was a transit line on either side of our spot. Because I was now on welfare I was also given a stipend for childcare. I found the perfect location for the children, The Children's Workshop. Azariah was enrolled full-time Alaisja and Ishaka would attend the after-care program.

After getting the children enrolled in their respective educational centers, I was left with time to seek employment. I applied to the McDonalds just down the way but was denied. I applied at the local grocery stores and was denied. I remembered the staffing agency that I'd worked for back in Jacksonville; Randstad. I logged into my computer and submitted my resume. Moments after my submission, I received a call from a woman with a voice that sounded like the underworld receptionist from Bettlejuice. "Hello, may I speak with uh Princess Booker?" I replied in my southern twang, "This is she. How may I help you?" "Ms. Booker, we've received your resume and would like to schedule you for an interview," the woman said. Hot diggity dog, I have an interview. I gathered my composure and accepted the invitation. "Well then Ms. Booker, we will need you here tomorrow morning by 10:30am. Please bring two copies of your resume along with identification and social security card." I approved and told her that would be there. "Thank you ma'am, I will see you tomorrow morning at 10:30am." The phone call ended. I feel to my knees and wailed praises unto the Lord. I was ecstatic.

Before picking up the children I made the biggest meal as if I were cooking for my entire family back in Florida. I collected the kids up from The Children's Workshop and told them of the good news as we strolled home. Alaisja was old enough to understand the importance of the news. Alaisja and I looked eyes for a brief moment and I could see her inner joy. She was proud of me. That's all I'd ever wanted.

Just as we entered our apartment I immediately turned on the music. Sounds from Maze featuring Frankie Beverly, Will Downing, Cassandra Wilson, Sade, Levert blared throughout the place. I beckoned the children into the kitchen where the found a spread of good eats. I even baked my household favorite chocolate cake. We ate good that night. My children ate until their little hearts were content. It was after all a celebration! Even though I'd only received an invitation to interview but somehow I knew that the job was mine.

The next morning when I rose, I my soul beamed with confidence. My children woke up just as excited as I was. Azariah was getting older, now much of toddler than an infant. She'd started to fall into the regime just as her siblings. As we prepared for our day, I noticed the lag. My babies didn't have their usual pep in their step. I stopped them to find out what the matter was. They wanted to stay home for the day. Alaisja walked over to me and asked if she could look after her siblings while I went to my interview. The sound of her voice allowed me to hear her heart. She wanted to show that she could look after her siblings while I was out. She wanted to help me.

God knows that I needed all of the help that I could get. After all Alaisja has been with me since I was seventeen years old. She witnessed my good and my bad. She witness the painful tears. She witnessed the bumps and the bruises. She heard my wailing cries unto the Lord in the midnight hour. She needed this moment. I told them that they could stay home while I went out. I finished making ready and gave myself the once over. I laid down the law before I left.

As I walked towards the bus stop I noticed that my shoes were not appropriate. I stopped by Fashion Cents and bought a pair of loafers. Now, I was ready. I made my way to the bus stop barely making it in time. I boarded the bus and showed the bus driver the address of my destination. He instructed me accordingly. I made my way to my destination meeting the face to match the woman's voice from the phone call. I checked in with her and she made copies of my documents just after notifying the recruiter of my presence.

I was met with firm handshake by a middle-aged white man that stood about 5'6". His name was John. I'd applied for a data entry position but after speaking with me John decided on a different position that he felt was better suited for me. It was an Administrative Assistant position at a local prestigious university. I was to report the following week at 9:00am for my new job. Well goodness gracious, I got a job! Glory be to God!

With a giddy soul, I went home to tell my children the good news! When I entered the door, I found my house intact and all of my children were settled. Alaisja had done her thing! I rewarded her that week with a new outfit from Fashion Cents. She deserved it and so much more. The kids and I spent the entire weekend carousing making memories.

The memory of waking that Monday remains fresh in my mind. I rose with a soul of thanksgiving and mind set on being great. Upon existing my bedroom, I couldn't believe my eyes. All of three of my children were up, fully dressed sitting at the dining room table eating their breakfast. I'd put on a crockpot of oatmeal the night before letting cook on low throughout the night. They were chatting away as I walked into the kitchen. Alaisja looked my way and through a proud smile she said, "Ma, you'd better get dressed for work or you're going to be late for your first." She was right, I had an hour and half to make ready, get the children to their respective places and me on the bus.

I put on my best office attire complimentary of Fashions Cents and wig compliments of Amazon. I pinned my hair up in a nice French roll to include a bang. My facial features enhanced with Fashion Fair's mineral powder and Beach Bronze lip gloss. I gave myself the once over and deemed myself ready for work. After dropping Azariah off to daycare I shuffled over to the bus stop just in time for its arrival. Upon boarding I showed the bus driver the directions of my destination and off we went.

Reaching my destination in awe of the campus and the distinguishing seasoned building. There I was, standing inside of one of America's oldest college campuses. Being the third college established in New England and the seventh in Colonial America, I couldn't believe it. I stepped into the building of which I had been assigned. Checking in with the receptionist was the most awkward experience. I was asked my name of which I gave. With a coy response,

"Princess is your name?" I asserted with, "Yes, Princess is my name. I am for the Administrative Assistant position in the Student Affairs Office." Astonishment was written all over her face. I was starting to feel like maybe I was in the wrong place. A moment of silence took place between the two us. "Well Princess, please have a seat." With hesitation, I took a seat.

"Hi there, Princess Booker right?" The question came from a 5'0" Hispanic young lady. "I'm Zora, follow me," she said. Before I could confirm my identity I found myself hot on her trail. We walked a small flight of stairs landing us at our goal. Zora continue to the office of Alicia Moran presented me and left us to our greetings. I stood before Alicia Moran which is the Director of Student Affairs and Lona Avallone, the woman I was assigned to work for. The engagement between the three of us was pleasant to say the most with the exception of complete disdain shown upon Lona's face. Lona advised that I would be working her and that she was my direct report. Lona and I exited Alicia's office together ending up in hers.

Engaging me in a manner of trying to figure and internally regretting her decision to not interview me before allowing me to start. I could feel the tension. The atmosphere in the small of office was thick as pig belly bacon. I pushed through it and so did she. I was presented with a list of duties that Lona had shortened in presence. She drew lines through a bunch of the listed duties using a black marker. I saw it but I didn't let it phase me. Lona showed me to my desk while pointing the supply closet out telling me where I could retrieve pen and paper.

Left alone to settle in become familiar with my isolated cubicle that sat just outside of Lona's office. The desk was a mess. Coffee stains, food crumbs, scattered documents, walls covered in multi-colored sticky notes; my brain could not function in such a space. I'd searched the supply closet for cleaning supplies and found Lysol wipes, a spray bottle of bleach along with a roll of paper towels. I commenced to cleaning and organizing not throwing out any of the scattered documents. I figured that the documents were important and came up with the idea to organize them by date. After arranging the documents, I had approximately six stacks that needed to put away. I went back to the supply cabinet to find a filing folders for each stack.

Now, my space was clear, I had nothing more to do. I sat contemplating on the list of duties provided to me by Lona just before my need for a cup of Joe kicked in. My nose led me to the pot of coffee that say centrally within the office. I didn't have my own cup so I had to use the paper cups provided. I didn't want to disturbed the others in the office but I could find the sugar. I turned to the left of me where a fashionably stylish red head sat with her gaze upon me. "Hello. Hi. Would you happen to know where I could find the sugar?" In a strong mom from the animated sitcom *Family Guy* voice she says, "Sure honey, it's over there." I followed the point of her finger and got the sugar.

Returning to my desk sipping on the nice hot cup of coffee mentally giving thanks to God for this opportunity; I realized that I was bored. I popped my head into Lona's door knocking slightly, "Hi, just checking in to see if there's anything you'd like for me do?" Without looking up Lona replied, "Sure, can you make copies of these for me?" I retrieved the papers from her and made the copies. My days went like this for weeks. Bored I was but I wouldn't complain. Soon answering the phone and taking notes for Lona were added on.

Though my days at work were unfulfilling to say the least, I found joy in the atmosphere. Midway through a call for Lona, Zora appears at desk with a purple sticky note that read, *You are my diversity* ending with a smiley face. Reading the note as I listened to the voice on the transmitting end of the phone puzzled me. *Her diversity, what did me?* Thinking about it, Zora and I were the only two minorities in the building let alone our department. I ended the call hurrying to rip the sticky note into shreds. A successful attempt to hide it and keep anyone from finding out. Inside I knew what she'd meant, so I thought.

The following week after getting my first cup of coffee I decided to stop by Zora office for change. Approaching the entrance I saw her plaque, Assistant Director of Diversity and Inclusion; how impressive. I couldn't wait to talk to her after reading that. "Zora, are you busy?" She replied, "No, come on in." We sat in her office for a brief friendly chat. Me, expressing how proud I was of her. She; admiring my perseverance. I'd made a new friend. Zora, suggested that we stepped out of office for lunch. I accepted her invitation and returned to my cubicle.

I wasted as much time as I could pretending to keep busy until I decided to long into the available computer and complete some my course work. Zora inspired me. If I ever wanted to graduate, I wanted it more after speaking with Zora. I couldn't wait to graduate and move towards my next degree. I had to finish. I put myself in gear and went to work. I was able to complete more work than anticipated before Zora arrived to retrieve me for our lunch date.

Zora and I took a nice stroll to a local café where we had Chicken Pesto Paninis over enjoyable chatter. Walking back to the office Zora asked how things were going with my job. Reluctant to speak frankly, I told her that I absolutely bored. I went on to say that Lona makes it a point to avoid me. I've asked for more things to do but she denied my requests on several occasions. Being there was becoming mind-numbing. Zora chuckled as I ranted on injecting to say, "Humph, I find that interesting because the woman before you had plenty to do. There was never a dull moment with her." I couldn't believe it. I told Zora about the list of duties Lona provided to me with the blacked out items. She was shocked.

Returning to the office, I sat thinking why would Lona not train me. What was her game? The documents! The documents that I'd organized by date when I first started. I pulled out those papers and did as my momma had trained me to do; I read everything. Astonished; I was completely astonished by what I'd discovered. I was just an Administrative Assistant. By God, I was the Clerkship Assistant to the Clerkship Coordinator of an Ivy League medical school. I froze momentarily until I grabbed my cellphone, ran out of the building to call my mom.

Sitting outside of the building dialing my momma's number, I had the jitters real bad. "Hello, hey girl how ya doin?" It was my mother's voice. "Momma, it's me." "Girl I know who it is," she said. "Momma, I need to talk to you about my job." I rattled on about how I got the job, the awkward silent treatment I received around the office, the diversity sticky, and now finding out the importance of my job and how "they" obviously didn't believe that I was capable of doing it. My momma was silent the entire time until I stopped. "Princess, when are you going to realize that you are Ivy League?" I tried to but, am ummm my way pass what she said. My momma wouldn't let me make excuses not to be who she knew I could be.

In tears, I re-entered the building wiping them away before I made it back to Student Affairs. I plopped into my seat internally processing my emotions. I prayed to God for answers, directions, a sign, something to help me. I heard a whispered voice encouraging me to read Exodus 23:20-33. I wasn't a big Bible reader although my prayer life had gotten a lot better than what it used to be. I guess it would after all the crap I'd been through. Exodus 23:20-33 in the Bible describes God sending an angel to prepare the way for the Israelites as they conquer Canaan. I printed that scripture and hung in my cubicle. I have never forgotten it. That scripture gave me motivation.

I went back through the documents and made notes. I'd learned how to prepare a presentation in school and used the teachings to help me create a beast of formatted data to present to Alicia and Luna. By the time I'd compiled my data and built of the courage it was time for me to leave for the day. Boy, was I anxious. I hid my folder in my desk and locked it until the next day. That was when I would make my move.

The entire bus ride home all I could think of was my presentation. I will show them what I'm made of. I was so deep in thought that I'd almost missed my stop. Dang it, if I'd missed my stop, I would have been late picking up the kids. I made to the children just in time to pick up the kids had I not I would have received a $200.00 fine. At $10.50 an hour, I couldn't afford that. Anywho, I made it which was all that mattered.

The kids seemed too excited to see me. Usually, I had to pull them away from the place. I didn't question it as I was uber excited to see them too. We made our way home but this day Ishaka was unusually chatty. That spiked my motherly antennas as he didn't talk very much. All he could talk about was Michael Jackson, little Michael Jackson at that! Apparently, he couldn't wait to get home to see the movie *The Jackson's, An American Dream*. They knew the movie was scheduled to air that night and couldn't wait to get home. Alaisja asked if we had popcorn at home. She told that she'd completed all of homework assignments while at The Children's Workshop. She even made sure Ishaka completed his homework. I was always impressed by my children. Azariah was now walking on her own and even talking. Life was looking up. We'd found happiness.

I didn't mention my presentation to anyone, I wanted to keep it to myself as not to jinx it. Plus, I wanted the kids to enjoy themselves not worrying about how my day was going. That night I watched those kids dance, sing and laugh. The atmosphere in our home was so full of life. They were able to be themselves without the stress of worrying about theirs and my safety. I was a barrel of water. It was a goodnight. I let them stay up past their bedtime to finish their movie. I took a nice hot bubble bath and let Calgon take me away. I finished my bath and joined the kids for the end of the movie. I sung with them until they went straight to sleep. I fell on my knees at my bedside to pray.

My prayers were simply me thanking God for His grace and mercy. I asked God to give me the strength that I would need to persevere and the confidence needed to get a successful presentation done.

Morning rolled in with the sun shining brightly through the windows of my home. The house buzzing with optimism. Everyone was up and at 'em; heading out the door with an increased amount of energy and self-awareness. I'd made to the office before the rest of staff; which was uncommon. I took advantage of the silence by playing a little Coltrane at a volume loud enough to fill the room yet low enough to respect the atmosphere. I started a pot of coffee using my brand of choice as they typical coffee did the job but the taste of it was sour. You needed lots of cream and spoons of sugar to mask it. I sat down at my desk reciting Exodus 23:20-33. I pulled out my presentation and prayed over it.

Logging into my computer to find an emailed communication from my school with subject line reading, *Graduation Eligibility*. Excitingly reading over the details, I found that I was one credit sort and had thirty days to complete it if I expected to graduate on time. Just as I found myself truly relaxed, the hustle and bustle of the staff coming into the office alarmed me. I immediately turned off the music and pleasantly greeted everyone. It seems as though they were all stuck in traffic due to a car accident which delayed their arrival to work. It sucked for them but worked for me.

I read over the cue cards created for my presentation. I don't know if what was the multiple cups of Folgers, my own self-sabotaging thoughts, or a combination of both, but I had the jitters. All of a sudden, I was flushed with fear. I knew that feeling all too well. It was there when I was a kid and needed to turn in my Alegbra homework and didn't think I'd done it correctly. So I didn't turn it in and received a failing grade. It was there every time I was called upon in church to sing and I would shy away thinking my voice didn't compare to the girls. It was there all the times I was presented with an advancing opportunity in my life and I would walk away thinking I wasn't worthy. What was that? Why was I like that? I hated that about myself.

It was do this thing or be out of a job as my temporary assignment was coming to an end. What harm could it do? No one believed in me anyway. Why not take the chance of actually succeeding in something other than having children. I made up my mind, I was going to do it. I drafted an internal email to both Alicia and Lona asking for a moment of their time to go over my job description versus what I am actually doing. I had ideas on how I could implement the duties of my actual to my daily copy making and note taking tasks. I clicked send; there was no backing out now. The email was now in the hands of the intended recipients.

"Princess, get in here!" I heard Lona's irritated voice call upon me. I stood to my feet with instant regret. I shook it off and entered Lona's office. "Close the door now," she exclaimed. "How dare you? Why would you send an email to Alicia? I am boss. You do not have the right to email her without going through me." Lona was in mid-reprimand when Alicia peeked in the door. "Hey ladies, got a minute?" Lona's tone of voice completely changed, "Sure Alicia we'll be right there."

There we all were again, the three of us in Alicia office just like on my first day. I sat as Lona stood. Alicia asked Lona to have a seat which she did. Alicia looked in my direction, "Princess, I was able to read your email and wanted to speak you and Lona about it." Lona attempted to apologize to Alicia for my behavior. Alicia told Lona that there was nothing to apologize for. She told us both that she'd wanted to hear what I had to say and complimented me on such a well communicated email. Lona was obviously surprised. You see the color red all over her face. I was pleased and asked if I could be excused to retrieve my presentation.

After retrieving my presentation and rejoined the ladies and started with saying, "I'm bored." I couldn't believe I'd said that out loud. But it was too late to turn back now. I had to power through. "Since I started I've been tasked with simply making copies of documents, getting coffee, answering the phone to simply transfer it to Lona. I have so much downtime." Alicia eyes widen and Lona cringed at words. "However, I've been going through the documents left in my desk by the previous occupant and realized that my job description was so much more. I've comprised a packet for you and Lona to look over. I've been in communication with some of the others here in the office who have assisted me in learning how to perform some of the duties listed. I know if given the opportunity, I am more than capable of fulfilling the actual role of Clerkship Assistant." Alicia smiled at me then asking, "Describe to me the role of the Clerkship Assistant." I jumped at the opportunity, "Please turn to page three of the packet."

I began with describing what medical school clerkships are. Medical school clerkships provide opportunities to practice evidence-based medicine, closely monitored by experienced physicians. Through these experiences, student can sharpen their skills in evaluating, diagnosis and treating patients. From there, I showcased my acquired knowledge as to when clerkships become available for medical students.

During the MS3 (third year of medical school) year, students are to complete core rotations (clerkships) in the following areas: Internal Medicine, Family Medicine, Surgery, Pediatrics, OBGYN and Psychiatry. At the end of each core rotation, students are required to take and pass a Subject Clerkship Exam; sometimes referred to as shelf exam. These exams are designed and licensed by the National Board of Medical Examiners. MS4 students have the opportunity to choose certain elective clerkships that are targeted to their passions. Core clerkships are 6-12 weeks long, while elective clerkships typically last between 4-8 weeks.

As it pertains to my role, I would do the following.

A Clerkship Assistant should help the director in designing, managing and evaluating a required clerkship in keeping with the School's overall competency based learning objectives, recommendations of the CCA and relevant national recommendations. Such assistance should be both practical and conceptual. The assistant should be able to substitute for the director in situations of the directors' absence. Specific areas of such support may include:

1. Assist in the scheduling of rotations, call, lectures, small group activities, etc.
2. Assist in grade compiling and calculation, including construction of individual student formative and summative evaluations.
3. Assist in writing and evaluating test questions.
4. Assist in the mid-clerkship feedback process and review of student logs of required clinical conditions.
5. Attend and participate in clerkship orientations.
6. Attend and participate in clerkship director meetings.
7. Assist with the development/implementation of new curricular items including, but not limited to new OSCEs, on-line education experiences, etc.
8. Assist the course director in preparing the Annual Inventory for Proposed Changes.
9. Attend and participate in the Student Review Panel Meeting.
10. Participate in leadership roles in SSOM educational activities, projects, task forces, etc. as opportunities arise.
11. When requested participate in important school events such as graduation.
12. Role model team work and inter-professionalism for the students
13. Participate in professional development activities
14. Assist the Clerkship Director in new school or clerkship initiatives and needs as they arise

This is what I rattled off and what they found on pages 3 and 4 of my presentation. Alicia couldn't believe it. She was amazed. Lona sat in her seat speech list. "Princess, you've done your research," Alicia stated. Alicia looked at Lona and asked her thoughts. Lona, sat silently scanning through the pages where she found an updated clerkship application, my suggestion to make the application available online. Lona finally spoke, "Well Princess, if you think you can do it let's give it a try." I wanted to cry and shout but I kept my composure. There will be plenty of time to celebrate. I'd won them over. I left out of Alicia's office with a new level of confidence; leaving the women to discuss whatever they needed to. As I pulled the door close behind me, I could hear Alicia ask Lona, "You really had her here all of this time making copies and fetching you coffee." I smiled and closed the door.

I let out silent praise to God; giving thanks for my new opportunity. I saw a yellow sticky note on desk from Zora asking me to come see her. Enthused to see what she wanted, I walked to her office. "Come in and have seat. Tell me what happened." Zora and I sat there and I went over the whole thing with her. She told me if I needed her help with anything, she was available. I returned to my desk and got started by logging into the company website accessible to me as the Clerkship Assistant. I performed my job with excellence ensuring all communicable documents were up to date. I contacted IT to ensure our website was updated and all application documents were available online for ease of access.

I'd come across other information that suggested that our school was a sister school to a medical school in Haifa, Israel. I researched the school to find their Clerkship Assistant and sent an introductory email. I received a response yet it was in written in Hebrew. At the Gmail was only offered to businesses and had a translation mechanism built in of which I used to translate and transcribe our communication. The exchange program between the two schools had lied dormant for over five years. My thought was to revive it. I ran it pass Lona, who didn't know much about it as she'd only been with the school for four years. Lona gave me the go ahead to move forward with my new project. I performed all of this still employed as a temp.

The catch was I'd made my presence valuable enough to be given the opportunity of permanent employment with the university. I received the offer letter of employment via email from Lona with Alicia and others in copy. I'd also received a call from the staffing recruiter of Randstad. He was elated after hearing all of my accomplishments and wished me well. I immediately signed off on the offer letter neglecting to read the full document. Continuing my new project of reviving the exchange program I was now in contact elite individuals within the university. The phone was no longer ringing for Lona; they were ringing for me. People wanted to talk to me about my ideas and meet me in person rather than simply emailing and phoning.

Those boring work days were now a thing of the past. I was booked, busy and in high demand. The day had come for to receive my first paycheck as a permanent employee. I came into the office bouncing and bubbly. My paycheck was waiting for me at my desk. I opened it immediately because I needed the money. Things were starting to get a little tight at home and the weather was in New England was starting to change. I pulled out the check and realized that I may have been overpaid. I went into Lona's office check in hand with a look of worry. "I can't cash this. I think something is wrong," I said to Lona. "Oh gosh, let me see." Lona looked over the check and asked me to follow her into Alicia's office. I was tore up and was ready to plead with them to get a new check that day.

Alicia looked at the check after Lona had handed it to her. The looked at one another smirking in the process. "Princess, what is wrong with the check," asked Alicia. It replied it was too much. Alicia asked me explain. To be honest I couldn't. "Princess, do you know how much you're being paid," Alicia asked. Honestly, I thought I was still making $10.50 an hour. "Princess, there's nothing wrong with the check. This is your salary and it's okay for you to deposit it into your bank account." I could believe it. I'd never seen so many zeros on any of payment checks. I've never made more than the $10.50 an hour. I asked Lona if I could take an early lunch break as I needed to deposit my check. Vystar was nowhere around and Navy Federal was over in Newport. I found a local branch and open a new account. I'd gone from $10.50 an hour to $25.00 an hour!!! Weeee Doggggy!

I worked my tail off, meeting every deadline and exceeding expectations. I was granted my own office, a slight pay increase and title change. I was no longer the Clerkship Assistant. I was now the International Clerkship and Exchange Coordinator. I still did certain tasks to assist Lona, but with the change in my duties it really took a lot off of her plate. Lona focused more on Credentialing and scheduling.

Due to the change in my finances and add perks of the job, I was able to enroll me children into private schools. Alaisja attended a local Quaker school learning Latin and advance core studies. Ishaka and Azariah were enrolled into the Catholic school just down the street from our home. Struggling to pay bills became a thing of the past. I'd decided to re-read The Secret and put into action the teaching of Bob Proctor. Bob gave a scenario of how to get out of debt by training your mind to see what you have versus what you owe. Taking heed to his message, I worked my way out of debt. I wasn't indebted to anyone or anything outside of my daily expenses. Needless to say, my credit score went up. I went from a low score of 428 to a high score of 720. This worked well as I'd now also obtained my AS in Human Resource Management.

This were definitely looking up for me until I received an unusual request from the universities Human Resources Department. I assumed that my application for tuition reimbursement triggered a flag of some sort. I forwarded the email to Lona and went to discuss it with her. She was aware of the request but didn't know what prompted it. I went over everything in mind. I am never late to work. I perform my job to the letter. I haven't had any issues with anyone in my department. What did she want?

Over next two weeks, I purposely delayed my meeting with HR. I didn't know what she wanted so I tried to ignore it as long as I could. Receiving an email from the Human Resource representative with Alicia in copy, I knew I couldn't hold off any longer. Alicia cleared my scheduled for the day and insisted that head over to the meeting. I walked over to the Human Resources Department Office; the building was ten blocks from Student Affairs. I made my up to the HR representative's office to be greeted by stubby black woman with cocoa skin, a short unkept 1990's Toni Braxton haircut, wearing a royal blue blazor… "Ms. Booker, I presume." I returned the greeting extending my right hand, "Yes, I'm Princess Booker and you are?" Smiling she gave me her. We talked back to her office and she went in. This woman had performed a background check on me and found all of my history; even the drug charge. That charge was not supposed to be there as I'd had my record expunged. As she rambled off all of the dirt she'd found, my mouth got dry. I was kind of shaken up. What was she aiming at? I didn't have to wait long until she asked, "So, is this all you?" I responded, "Yes, that is all me." She was shocked that I admitted to it. As if? She then followed with the most insulting question, "So with such a colorful past, why do you think we should continue to allow you (strong emphasis on the word you) to work at our prestigious institution?" In mind, I was laying her out but verbally, I explained that having such a colorful past had prepared me to face the day to day challenges of being a minority in a predominately white institution. That in spite of my past, I'd rose up in the ranks within my department and far exceeded any and all expectations. Not only had I become an asset in Student Affairs but my work, dedication along with my colorful past had financially changed the dynamic of the university's exchange program. I continued and ended with the staff and students at this prestigious university had become reliant upon my knowledge, my willingness to assist, my availability and I've opened up opportunities for our medical students to experience foreign clerkships under the universities umbrella. That shut her up. The meeting ended and I returned to work never to hear from HR again; with the exception of them signing of my request to be reimbursed for my college courses.

Periodically throughout my tenure, I would still wonder why I had to have that meeting with HR. It hit me; darn it Lona, you did this! Lona had submitted a request for Human Resources to investigate me. She was trying to find a way to get me out of there. Since day one, I've done all that she asked me to do and more. I didn't lollygag. I was pleasant yet stern. I adapted to the upper class environment. I took the racist shots to my character, accent, and hair. I didn't react to the unpleasant looks. I kept my head held high but I was always humble. I later found out that sometimes that some people will envy you simply because you're you.

During my time at the university I continued to make an impact with students and staff alike. The winter months were isolating for me and the children as we didn't get out much. I'd started to drink a little more than usual which later turned into a coping mechanism. Nostalgia started to set in the more I would talk to my family and friends back in Florida. The kids and I needed more space so I found us a place on the Eastside of Providence. It was closer to my job as it was centralized just outside of downtown Providence. I could literally walk to work.

One of my daily strolls to work, I decided to stop by a local Dunkin Donuts for an iced coffee when I met a tall light and handsome broad shouldered, strong physique brother name Tyrone M. We exchanged pleasantries and numbers. Tyrone and I got to know one another and decided to make a go of it. He was like a knight in shining armor and I was his Princess; his damsel in distress. Tyrone appreciated my hard work, dedication and overall character. Our relationship was a passionate one. After introducing him to my children, I knew he was the man for me. Tyrone played a major role in our lives. Whenever the chips were down, he would pick up the pieces. I loved him.

Many days I would arrive at work to find boxes of chocolate from Shari's Berries, beautiful floral arrangement, fruit baskets, etc. Tyrone was such a romantic; slowly sweeping me off my feet. I would periodic text messages from Ty instructing me to of a time to be ready for a plan event/date. It felt good to be loved and cared for. He amazed my heart. The children loved him and still do. But I slowly came to learn that sometimes love just isn't enough.

The summer came around and my mom wanted to visit us. I was excited to see her as it had been such a long time. I told Ty all about it. He was just as excited as I was. He really wanted to me my mom and that made me nervous. My mother was a great woman, yet extremely complicated and a little eccentric. She was an acquired taste but people seemed to really love her. For me, there were time that I loathe her presence as it was easy to read that she didn't much care for me either. Even still, I was happy to have my mother around she was my closet friend and at times my most formidable opponent.

It was 5pm on a Friday, 95 degrees in the city. My mother arrived at the airport. Tyrone and I hurried to the arrival gate; there we greeted her. Briefly introducing the two, which they actually hit it off. Of course they would, Ty was such a gentleman and his smile would lighten the heaviest of hearts. Carrying my mom's bags to the car; the two of them just couldn't stop talking. It was great! They really got along.

We'd arrive to my place and right off; my momma's eyes should her thoughts. She did not approve. Apartment living in Providence wasn't anything like Florida. No one should expect that it would be.

We lived a quiet neighborhood where all of the people knew one another in one way or another. There were no major disturbances outside the occasional rhythm of the night parties held by my Latino neighbors every Friday. I figured that once she got a chance to settle in she'd see the beauty that I saw. Wishful thinking.

The kids met us at the door. They were all over their grandma. My mom made her through the wave of excited bodies and plopped her suitcase onto my dinner table. Tyrone and I looked at one another with the eye of question. She unzip her suitcase just to pull out frozen precooked collard greens, froze southern brown gravy, and her special pound cake. I was excited and a little embarrassed of what was happening there. I'd guess she actually listened when I once told her that I had to purchase collard green in Rhode Island by the pound not by the bunch. Tyrone had to leave as it was his weekend with his boys. He was never late for them and he always kept his word. I loved that about him.

After being with us for two weeks, my mother's perception of our new home didn't change much. Hell, I think the longer she stayed the more she hated it. I was constantly working. The kids had strict learning schedules accompanied by sports and hobbies. She didn't agree with my parenting style; she made sure I knew it. I brushed of her indirect sarcastic remarks but honestly all of the negativity wore me out. I didn't stand up to her; I simply retreated into my bedroom. The kids were happy that's all that mattered.

Tyrone came with a fantastic idea to take us on a site seeing tour and dinner. He gave me the itinerary and I made sure that we were all dressed for the festivities. We had a ball all day; ending the day with dinner at a lovely restaurant. The waiter presented Ty with the bill, my mother takes a glance at the bottomline and says, "Hell, I could've made all this food and ya'll could have paid me that money." With my napkin, I covered my shameful face. The kids got a good laugh though, so did Ty. I didn't find it funny at all because I knew what was coming next. My mom had a habit of hitting any man I dated up for money. Big or small, it didn't matter she just asked them for money. Her sense of entitlement to have some part of what was mine; the freaking nerve. I never said anything to her about it. I did express my thoughts of her actions to my therapist.

It was time for her to go! I wanted her out of my house and back in Florida. Her constant judgement made me cringe. "You act just like a white woman." "You cook just like a white woman." "You got my grandkids living all the way up here treating them like they white" "You gon' make Alaisja turn gay going to that all girl's school." "She gon' be a bulldagger if you keep letting her play basketball." Damn! I just wanted her to hush and let us live. Mind you, she said all of these things around my children. I needed a drink!

Tyrone and I dropped my mother off to airport's departure gate. I hugged her briefly and she went on her merry way. As we drove back into the city, the car ride was awkwardly silent. Ty was usually pretty chatty but something seemed off. Ty asked me if I were hungry. I nodded to say yes. We found a quaint little Portuguese restaurant to dine. Over lunch, Ty broke up with me. "Princess, I don't know if I can do this anymore." I didn't know what he was talking about. Perplexed I sat hearing him say, "Your mom told me everything." When did he and mom talk? What the hell was *everything*? The puzzle was starting to come together nicely. I couldn't believe. My momma had told this man all about me being molested as child, how I was a stripper, how I'd been kidnapped, the domestic violence... she even told him about the time she had me committed into a mental asylum!

I'd told Tyrone some things but not everything. Telling a man that I been raped backfired the first time I did. Alaisja's father called me damaged! I vowed to never tell another man about that; what purpose would it serve? Knowing all of that along with the graphic details she painted was too much for him. I understood his decision yet asked him to take me home. Why would she do that? She always ruined things for me. Anything that brought me a small piece of joy, she stepped in and crushed it. I never asked my mom about this. I just went on with life drowning all of the pain with several glass of rum.

CHAPTER 21

They Always Come Home to Roost

The pain of my past lingered heavy amidst the accolades. No matter how far I ran, the pain was there. No matter how many times I made myself over, the pain was there. No education, no praise, no silence could take the pain away. Certain wounds never heal, I came to learn that. The dreams were back; they never left. This moment in time, something must've triggered me. I started having memories of my abuse that began with dreams and then formed into day terrors. I could be walking in the grocery store all of a sudden, a horrific scene would pop into my head. One memory was of the first time, he molested me. Why now?

His sister gave me a bath and dressed me for bed. I attempted to put on my Care Bear underwear and she wouldn't let me. "No, you don't need to sleep with those on," she said. I loved her and felt safe with her; so I listened. When we exited the bathroom, she led me into his room and told that is where I would sleep that night. I knew him just as I knew her; they were like family. The room was so dark with only the television playing; Yo' MTV Raps. I wanted my brother. Something inside of me knew I was in trouble with no way out. He came upon me. All I could hear were The Jets singing *You've found out, I've got a crush on you*. Why is this happening? Why are these memories actively in my brain?

The memories got so bad until I started having physical attacks. My body had started remembering. They were starting to overtake me. Periodically, demonizing flashbacks would haunt my days, which made it hard to work, hard to parent, hard to live. Standing at the stove cooking breakfast; as I scrambled the eggs my vaginal area went into shock. I fell hard to the kitchen, cuddling myself. Alaisja found me there, crying and moaning in pain. The agony; the shame. My daughter had to see like this. Alaisja helped me to my feet and into a chair.

"Momma, what's wrong?" I didn't know what to say other than the truth, "He hurt me…" I managed to say through the tears. She held me, squeezing tightly. I snapped back into reality to the smell of burning eggs. I attempted to stand and found my legs weren't quite working as they should. "Momma, I got it. Just sit momma, I got it."

I asked Alaisja to find my cellphone. I had to schedule an emergency appointment with my therapist. Hoping and praying that she could me to figure out what was happening to me and why. Upon dialing the number, I was immediately batched to the office's voicemail. I left a message in desperation begging her to return my call. I needed to lay down but first I needed a drink. I prepared myself a stiff rum and diet coke with a twist of lime. I advised Alaisja to keep an eye on her siblings while I recuperated. I hug her slightly as I rushed off to my bedroom. There were way too many days like this as life went on.

The elixir of alcohol, avoidance and work became a part of my daily life. Each time I would experience body memories or painful nightmares, the more I drank. I became a functioning alcoholic. Slowly falling into depression fighting to live long enough for my children to remember me and long enough to establish a nest egg for them after I was gone. Therapy seemed to be working temporarily. After each session, I left a little wiser to my childhood traumas. I'd established a baseline connection to my poor adult decisions. Some of things that came out during our talks really pissed me off. I'd started to hate certain family members and resent all of them.

They knew what was happening to me as a child and no one stopped it. They all just went about life as normal never mind the destructive behaviors. Lies! It was all lies! I had to get a handle on all of this. Imagine taking your children for a walk to get ice cream and fainting on side of the road. Waking to find your three children sitting next to you in tears begging you to wake up. That happened and it could never happen again. They didn't deserve that. They lived through my suffering; withdrawing from them mentally. Shutting down emotionally. That was not fair to them. I prayed to God asking Him to heal me; take away the memories. They were crippling me as a person, these thoughts. The memories didn't stop, they only became a little more manageable. I'd made the Dean's List and was on my way to graduating with my B.A. in Accounting.

The more intrusive the memory was, the harder I went in school and at work. If I was ever going to escape my past, I had to make more money. In order to make money, I had to become better educated. The more education I acquired the further from my roots I would go, taking my children with me. I became highly successful in my career. I was an exemplary student, graduating with the top of my class. I was on power journey; nothing could stop me.

One morning in September of 2014, at working scrolling Facebook listening T.I.P. I came across a post that read, "Please pray for my Auntie Cynt." One of my cousin Snookie's baby mother's had made the post. I commented, "What's wrong with my momma and why has no one called me." Grabbing my cellphone, I called my mother's home and heard my granny's voice. "Hello…" "Granny, what's wrong with my momma? Why didn't anyone call me?" My granny slowly responded, "Princess, she's fine. We didn't want to bother you." Bother me? Why would calling me to tell me that something was wrong with my momma be a bother to me? Anyhow, the conversation continued ending with my grandmother giving me the number of the hospital where my mom was admitted.

I called the hospital and was transferred to my mom's room. My mother's voice was so weak. She wasn't herself; she sounded drained. "Momma, what's wrong? Are you okay?" She explained to me that she'd had a mild heart attack. Working at the medical school had taught me a little about medical terminology. There's nothing mild about a heart attack. My mom had experienced a myocardial infarction. Which is a partial blockage of a coronary artery that limits the amount of oxygenated blood reaching the heart muscle. Mild heart attacks can cause less damage to the heart muscle and some patients may not experience any symptoms. However, all heart attacks are serious.

I didn't want to press her so I ended the call with I love you, Ma and I'll be home soon. I called her every day after that even when she got out of the hospital. I'd informed my children of their grandmother's situation. It ate them up inside. I could help but worry. My mom wasn't out of the hospital for more than week, until she her seizures started up again. They were coming more often than usual since she had the brain surgery back in 1997. My worries turned into fear and prompted me to resign from my position at the university. I had to get to Florida. It was time for us to go back home. Looking back, that was one of the most irresponsible moves of my career.

Not looking back, I cashed in my retirement savings and made my way back to Florida using my Housing Voucher. Yes, I was still on Section 8. The State of Rhode Island didn't kick me off even after examining my income. My housing counselor was extremely proud of me and showed me favor; allowing to me get my life on the right track. The housing authorities across America have a program for individuals receiving Section 8 assistance called HCV Transferring (Porting).

The process begins with the recipient notifying their current housing counselor that they want to move. In my case, it was me wanting to relocate to Jacksonville, Florida from Providence, RI. The initial housing authority must then forward certain importance documents to the importing housing authority. The process takes about two to four weeks. I waited the four weeks as it gave me time to clear out my office, say good-bye to friends, pack and hire a moving company and withdraw the kids from their schools. My children were ecstatic. Alicia tried to talk me out of leaving. Just like we flew in to Providence, we flew out.

We stayed with my family for the first two weeks realizing that my mom's entire hospital stint was all ploy. She'd faked the whole thing just to get my attention. She knew if I thought she wasn't well, that I wouldn't waste any time moving back home. These are her words not mine. I couldn't believe it! It was too late to turn back now. Did she even realize all that I'd given up? She didn't care as long as she got what she wanted from me. Those two weeks were dreadful for me. Totally accelerating for the kids; but torturing for me. I needed a drink.

I called up my homegirl Zhane and told her the good news! I was back in town and ready to prowl around. We decided to grab a drink at the local watering hole, *Jim's Place* for old time sake. My style of dress had drastically change and I was in desperate need of a rock'em sock'em dress and come catch me if you can heals. I raided Zhane's closet until she put something stylish together for me. I was ready for our night out. It had been so long. Zhane and I partied hard that night. Keeping cute and seductive was our motto. I needed for the moment to last a lifetime. A sweet brief moment of relief; away from the stress.

My children and had settled into the City of Jacksonville. I'd found schools for the prior to our relocation. I'd also applied for a position at the University of North Florida's Alumni Hall which I landed. I'd fallen into the mix of work, parent, play, love and party. It seemed like a healthy balance as the demons of my past were at bay. The nightmares were subdued by glasses of cognac and sleep aids. I'd become comfortable with our routine. The kids adjusted well enough into their lives. I walked a tight rope with my family interactions as being around them made me love them and hate them at the same time. I remembered the good times and did my best to deny the bad times without allowing my children to be poisoned.

It's something about the air here in Jacksonville that brings about nostalgia and makes you want to take of helter-skelter out of the city. I enjoyed the liberation of breaking the run of the mill cycle of life of living in Providence. I did miss the relaxation of it all. Working at UNF was cool but it was nothing like the prestigious institution in New England. The pay sucked and I was treated like I didn't belong. My co-workers were older white women from the South that had landed their jobs by legacy not education. My work was constantly challenged amongst my peers. My supervisor didn't stick up for me. There were time when my lizard brain wanted to smack the hell out of all of them. Making a note of the changes I'd made in my life allowed me to step back and consider the challenges as a chance to learn and grow professionally.

The more I ate their punches, the more they found new weapons. The last straw was when I walked into work one morning as was asked to come review a spreadsheet. I put my purse and keys down on my desk and walked into the office of my direct report, meeting the glaring faces of two old betties grinning while playing Clarence Carter's Patches. "Hey Princess, ya' ever heard this song before?" I had not but I sure as hell as listening. "My mammy used to play this song all the time when I was little girl." Did she just say *mammy*? She went on and on about how she had a black mammy who used to clean her childhood home. Apparently, their housekeeper was also her nanny. She also mentioned that her mammy didn't know how to read or write so she taught her. The other woman stood there laughing and watching me to see if I would have a reaction. I didn't give her the satisfaction. I simply said, "Great song! I'm sure your mammy would be proud of you. Especially after teaching her to read and write. It was tough being black in America back then. It surely paved a way for me. Just look at me in a lead Accounting position at such a beautiful university, holding multiple degrees. It's amazing how far we've come as a community; yet, there's still so much more work to be done." The look on their faces was priceless. You would've thought I'd killed their dogs or something. "Great song by the way," I said as I walked away begrudgingly.

I faced their torment daily for three whole months. As they were hell bent on making a mockery of me; I was slowly gathering intelligent information about each and every one of them. I couldn't wait for the opportunity to use my ammunition. They were the first to fire shots. Wounded by their targeted campaigns I was. As the saying goes, a weapon may be formed it against you; it may even be used… yet it will not prosper. I'd lived to fight another day.

And the day had come. Ishaka was starting to show signs of ADHD which would constantly land him in the principal's office and constant calls to me from the school. One of the bitter betties decided to pop her head in my office with another inappropriate *black joke*. I'd enough! My response to was bringing up her back wood mountain West Virginian roots. Identifying her out of wedlock pregnancy and her first marriage to 3rd cousin sent her reeling out of my office. Professionally speaking, my response may have been a bit harsh and out of line. I knew that I would have to pay for it later and pay I did. She went to HR on me and reported that she didn't feel safe around me. I was given the opportunity to respond but I could tell the decision was already made; I was fired. Dammit why did I do that? Initially regretting my decision and then realizing the art of war was to be played like an intense game of chess. Never allow your emotions to show. Always remain in control of your emotions. I needed a drink!

It didn't take me long to find another job at a different college. It was tough discussing my career challenges with my friends as everyone either worked in remedial positions, had their own businesses or they just weren't close enough to me to receive my dump of personal data. The only friend that I had who understood me lived in Texas; Chiquita Strong. I admired her tenacity as mother, a woman, a career driven mogul and friend. She understood the challenges in my life and didn't make feel as if I was putting on airs. Chiquita was the first person to encourage to write my story. I can never thank her enough for believing in me when I felt no one in world saw me.

I'd met a wonderful guy Jeffery is his name. Jeffery was this high powered executive for a prominent global company. We met at a bar in a nightclub; me admiring his cuff links and he admiring the way I wore my watch. Jeffery and I hit it off; we were kindred spirits. Him being a divorcee. A dad of two successful adult children. Both of us carrying dark passengers linked to our past. We were both searching for the meaning of life. You would think that after moving away, changing patterns, embracing the pathways to success as outlined by the US standard of living; the apple pie of it all… that we would be happy. There was lingering emptiness that we played upon when were together. I didn't love him and he didn't need for me to love him. The companionship brought us closer and what ultimately drove us apart.

Jeffery needed someone to take care of; why not a wounded woman in need of someone to care for. He didn't need to cuddle with me and I hate cuddling. He didn't crowd my space and try to engage me sexually. I didn't have a high sex drive. We got along well; until we didn't. My nightmares slowly crept in. The alcohol was not enough to silence the noise. I would have fits of rage on drunken benders. The chaos was too much for Jeffery who needed calm and regime. He would do his best to comfort with me nights out on the town, flowering, candy, baecations and family time. The lavish life he gave me was needed but it wasn't enough to release my traumatic shackles. I couldn't get out my own way.

Jeffery came to me with a proposal; a real proposal. Marry him, allow him to adopt my children and move with him to Dubai. I knew it meant to be. I'd always wanted to visit the Burjj Khalifa which is in Dubai. I was ready to pack my things and go. But, the children. How would this affect my children? They were much older now and had already been through enough. This was a chance for us to really live. I never believed in a single parent household. Can it be done? Sure. Should be done? Absolutely NOT! Children deserve a home with two parents, loving and caring for them with the financial means to set them apart of from the rat race. I wasn't given that and look how I'd turned out. I wasn't a complete mess but I sure as hell wasn't my best self. That's it we're moving to Dubai with Jeffery. Bye-bye agony.

I took the kids out for pizza and a little fun at a local carnival. They rode the rides until their little hearts were content. With a belly full of cotton candy, pizza and soda; I'd decided to sit them down and discuss our new move. I actually thought that they would be excited. They loved Jeffery. Upon delivering the news to my babies, I could see the light in their eyes dwindle. "What's wrong you guys?" They were reluctant to tell me their thoughts. I pried and they spilled their guts. They didn't want to move. They were happy being with their grandmother. They loved their cousins. They enjoyed going to church functions. They even liked their schools. Dammit! I can always go to Dubai. I could even find another Jeffery. I couldn't disappoint my children; not again.

I called Jeffery and gave him the news. He was gone two days later. Months had gone by until I'd finally heard from him. We Skyped and he told me all about his new life in Dubai. I held back tears as I only wanted him to see me happy for his new adventure in life. We never spoke again after that. I often think of him. Nostalgia.

After Jeffery there was Pip. Pip equally spoiled me. Pip adored me and I him. He was fun and bit mysterious. Pip was an Officer with the US Navy stationed in Mayport. He had a vigorous work schedule as did I but we always made time for one another. Pip was big on giving flowers and candy. His alternatives were modern appliances. I didn't mind as I needed them! Pip ensure my carnal needs were met but something was missing. I couldn't quite place my finger on it until I did. Pip was married. Have mercy, I am dating a freaking married man. I cannot be dating a married man. That is amoral. Karma is real and one day I just might have a husband. I wouldn't dare want my husband to cheat on me let alone buy her expensive gifts, travel with her, play with her children and make plans with her. I felt horrible but

Pip always reassured me that it was me that he wanted. I fell for it; hook line and sinker.

Such a fool to believe I was everything he needed. I'd taken a part-time job as a waitress at Olive Garden during for Winter holidays. I wanted the kids to have a big Christmas. We'd never really celebrated holidays but they deserved it. They were all kicking butt in school and at home. One afternoon after being scheduled to work a double, I was in the swing of things making ready to take my first break. Just then, the hostess say a two top in my section. It was two beautiful sistahs.

Tired on wanting to get off my feet just for me, I shook the feelings and pleasantly approached the lovely ladies. "Hi, welcome to Olive Garden. My name is Princess. I will be your server this afternoon." Just as I'd completed my introduction, I realized that I'd just identified myself. One of the two beautiful sistahs happened to be Pip's wife. I knew as I looked upon her gaze fixated on me. Her hair, her skin, her size, and the gap between her upper two front teeth… she looked like me and I looked like her. Pip had a type. The wife didn't make a scene. I walked away from the table and brought back two glasses of water. "It must be nice living off someone else's husband while you work as waitress." One of the women said. I don't know which one said it as this moment was a very awkward. I smiled and said nothing to my defense. I couldn't defend my actions. I was knowingly sleeping with a married man. I waited on them as if they were normal customers without a hidden agenda. I took their childish banter paying it no never mind as it was circumstantial data with the exception of me sleeping with her husband. They paid for their food and even let me a tip of two cents. I called Pip and told him that it was over. I've never told him what happened. I simply called off the facade of love and moved on.

I didn't date much after that. I spent my time with my children and self-help books. I attended countless seminars targeted to seek within to find true happiness. The more I sought within for my happy place I kept running into places with slivers of light. My prayer life had dwindled down to nothing. Each day I got to face a new day with a smile and a painful heart. I'd stopped letting people get too close me as I didn't want them to see what lurked in the shadows. No one would see the tracks of my tears. Hiding so much pain caused stress and the stress developed into anger. I ran as far as I could within only to end up in the same place. My workload had taken up any extra time I had to let my hair down. The kids suffered at my hand. I can never take that away. Beating my children when I was in such a dark hole is a huge regret. I didn't like who I was becoming. Spiraling; it was becoming too much to handle now with so much to lose.

Scrolling on Facebook was such a needed distraction. I could post the most intriguing clichés and acquire empty accolades that fed my starving ego. Another mask. I was able to be noticed without being seen. Cloak and dagger, the intrigue of getting to know me and me hiding my true secrets. Enticing myself with the receipts of others often wondering what were they hiding. It was a show and tell of misleading appearances. The dance of borrowed wit. The manipulation of a beautiful life. The need to know that the grass could be greener putting us all on autopilot without even knowing. A true erudite mind would be appalled. But, such is life.

All in all, I came across and arousing photo of an old childhood friend, Leo. A face I hadn't seen since I was about eight years old. He looked the same but distinguished and well built. He accepted my friendship on the little blue app. We engaged coy flirtatious post and direct messages, then swapped contact numbers. It was on from there. He vacationed in Birmingham, Alabama and invited me to visit him. I took the opportunity which turned into a mating ritual. We continued this way for weeks on end. Enjoying the aloof posture of our distance. It wasn't romance but it sure as hell was fun. It took the nightmares away if only for a moment in time.

Alaisja was due to graduate soon and had become a tad rebellious. I'd kept the restraints on too long and she was fighting for her own freedom. She'd become a caged bird of my rules fears, requirements and unemotional love. She couldn't take me anymore. She ran away! My entire world stopped. What had I'd done? At least my mom gave me a sense of freedom even if it was fake. Where was my child? Is she safe? How can I get her home? I called my mom and she rushed to my house, finding me in a mess of wistfulness. I blame myself. I saw Alaisja's cries for help but I ignored them believing that she had be tough. Alaisja had to be strong; because I was weak. My mind swooned with regretted, agony, thoughts about what was happening to her, what could happen to her. I needed her back. I fainted.

Coming to was Leo, Ishaka, Azariah, grandparents and my mom. I hadn't called the cops. I had resources that could do what needed to be done faster and more effective than the police. My brain kicked in to high gear which prompted me to contact Kirk advising him of the situation. He confirmed and assured me that he would bring her home to me. Kirk didn't find Alaisja; Leo did. He'd brought my child home. Who was he? Alaisja return home was taxing unraveling the ties that had bond us. I couldn't reach her. I didn't want to admit that my child had become addicted to some street drug unbeknownst to me. All the times that I'd thought she was simply too tired because of her strenuous school course load; AP Classes, college courses, lead choir singer, junior church accountant, political assistant, big sister, older daughter... it was too much; the child was experimenting with drugs.

She didn't want to leave with me anymore. She wanted to move with my mother. I concede to her request but my momma wasn't having it. With a firm assertion she demanded that Alaisja remain in my home and that we work it out. I put all of my issues aside to adhere to her. Alaisja didn't want me. That was the first time my child had rejected me. I wasn't prepared for it. I could take it. I pushed through the pain and continued the routine of this happy home when the walls all around us had started to collapse. I'd given Alaisja all that a child could want. A nice home, designer clothing, food on the table, an upper echelon education, love; yet something was missing. I later found out from her that the void was my lack of empathy and emotion. In order for me to build a life I had to become numb in certain places or life would have really been hell for them.

Leo had decided on an extended stay. He had family in the area and he didn't want to leave me. He saw me spinning out of control and wanted to be my strong tower. I wasn't eating like I should, so I'd lost so much weight. I didn't want to go outside and had started closing myself off. I couldn't hide the depression any more although I tried. I losing my grip. I attempted to shake things by taking a note from my past; dress up really nice, explore the night life and have a few drinks. I grabbed the keys to my cousin's rental car and left the house. I'd bought me a bottle of Remy 1738 and received an empty red cup from the cashier so I could pour my troubles as I drove. There I was with a full cup of Remy Martin driving tears flowing down my face, praying for God to take away my troubles, heal my daughter and protect my kids from me. I pulled over alongside of the road in an unfamiliar neighborhood, hand and head upon the steering balling my eyes out, crying out to God to fix it all. After a moment, I gathered my composure and decided to head home. My cellphone rang; it was Leo asking me to come home. I assured him that I was in route.

As I hung up the phone, the most graphic memories flooded my brain. That image of him on top of me as that song by The Jets played loudly. Being tied to a bed with home coaching the neighborhood boys on how to have sex with a girl. My laying there with a face full tears and no one coming to help me. My little brother cowering in the corner watching everything happening to me without the strength to help me. Me; reassuring my brother that it was all okay; what they were doing to me wasn't hurting me when it was. Pain in vaginal area pierced me like a thousand needles, I was unable to drive. Blinded by the memories; I couldn't see the road before me. In a state of shock and the wanting for it all to end, I drove the car off a cliff crashing into a ravine. I could feel the car slowly sinking into this large body of water.

The voice was back; guiding me once again. "Princess, wake up." Through a clouded mind, I could hear the voice. I came to. "Princess, unlock your seat belt now." I did. "Princess, if you do not open your door now, you won't be able to." I opened my door. Water came rushing through the car. "Princess, you have to get out now." The voice spoke with intensity. I scooted myself out of the car. I exited the vehicle in complete darkness. I could not see my hands it was so dark; no lights anywhere. I could feel the pressure of the car as it sunk. "Princess, you have to move now or you'll be taken down along with the car." I backed away and immediately felt afraid. I could hear the animal sounds all around me. I was in Florida… freaking alligators. I had to get out of there but which way was out? "Princess, turnaround and put out your arm." I extended my left arm clinging onto my new but now ruined baby blue Dooney & Burke purse.

I did as the voice directed which ultimately led me to an embankment. As soon as my hand touched the wall of earth, I felt a hand wrap around my around pulling me up. I don't know what happened after that all I know is I woke laying on the street with an elderly white woman hoovering over me. "Thank God, you're alive," she said. After hearing that, I must've passed out again. When I woke up again, I was laying in the woman's room on her sofa with a huge dog standing over me. The woman brought me a hot cup tea which I reluctantly sipped. Although she'd saved my life, I didn't know her.

Noticing my state of being the woman shared a small piece of advice; "Your life is worth living. God has a bigger plan for you. Whatever made you do this, you have to let it go and move on." I heard her but I didn't. All I could think about was how I was going to tell my cousin what happened to her car. How was I going to sneak into the house pass my children? "Hey young lady, call your mother. You need to call your mother." Oh gosh, I had to call my momma. The woman handed me the phone and I dialed my mother's number. I didn't realize the time but it was obviously late going into the morning. My mom answered and the woman took the phone from my weak hands. I could hear her explaining her account of what had happened.

I passed out again then waking to my mother's voice and seeing my grandfather's face. They came for me and took me home. That ride home was filled with my mother's tears crying out to God on my behalf. My grandfather cried begging me to understand how much I was loved. I heard them but my mind was clouded. They wanted to know from me how I survived. I could only tell them that I heard a voice.

Upon arriving to my house, my mom and grandfather walked me in. I was greeted by the sad faces of my children and the crumbling face of Leo. He felt like he'd let me down. My children thought the incident was their fault. Everyone was taking responsibility of my action but me. I just wanted to get out of the wet clothes, bathe and go to sleep; that is what I did. I shut everyone out. I was never charged with leaving the scene of an accident as my family had cleaned up my mess. No one spoke of this again.

I picked up and on with life but with first comforting my children the way that I could reassuring them that nothing that I've done was ever their fault. I explained to them that I would be better. Being better meant not addressing the real issues just try to prevent more from arising. That I did to the best of my abilities. Two months later, my mom was found nonresponsive on the floor of a gas station bathroom. She had an aneurysm that laid dormant and it burst killing her. The cashier at the location found her and phoned the police. The arriving officer called to inform me of the news. I heard him say the words, "she was found nonresponsive" at least three times but I could not compute. I asked him where she was and he told me that they were taking her to Beaches Baptist Medical Center. I asked him how he found my number; he told me that it was on the screen of her phone as she was attempting to call me; Princess-Daughter.

Hanging up the phone, I immediately ran to my room to get Leo. He was just getting out of the shower still dripping with water. "Get your clothes on. They've found my mom nonresponsive. They are taking her to Beaches Baptist." He hurried getting dressed. We jumped in the car and made our way towards the location. Nearer the location my cellphone rung; it was one of my cousins advising me that they were life-flighting my mom to Baptist Medical Center-Downtown. We made a b-line and made it there to find my entire immediate family. I searched for my brother finding first my children. I can't remember who picked them up from school for me. I hugged my children and held them closely, reassuring them that their grandmother was going to make it. I could hear the chatter in the room not really able to make out what everyone was saying.

My cousin Laiana approached me face of tears and welcoming arms whispering in my ear, "Princess, the doctor is looking for you." I found the attending physician standing outside of my mother's overly crowded hospital room. "You're Princess," he asked. I nodded in agreeance. He walked me into the room all I could see was my mother lying there connected to life saving machines, my grandmother's broken face and my brother's never ending gaze. I knew what was going on but I couldn't accept it. I slowly walked closer to my mother's bedside, looking upon her like that. My heart sanked but I had to try. I leaned in to her and begged her to wake up. I promised her that I would never leave her again. I asked God to allow her to live; I needed her. She couldn't be dead; not yet. We had so much to say to one another. We had so much life to live together. It was going to get better; I could make it better. All God had to do was wake her up.

My aunt Michelle stood closely at my side. It was body that kept me from falling. I could her praying to God for me. Why was she praying for me? I didn't need the prayers; my momma did. Every childhood memory of my momma came rushing back. Her beauty, her joy, her pain, her struggles, her victories; her face. The doctor called for me. He needed to inform me that my mom was actually deceased and that the lifesaving machines weren't doing any good; it was time to pull the plug. How could I do that? Standing there with the doctor, I heard the sobs of another. I glanced over to find my mother's brother; my uncle Alfred. I hadn't seen him since I was teenager; before I was pregnant with Alaisja. He'd heard everything the doctor said to me. Brokeness was all over him. Jesus so much pain. My uncle gave me a look that confirmed what the doctor had said. I took his cue and advised the doctor to pull the plug on my momma.

February 22nd, 2016, my mother died. It is not a day that passes that I do not long for her. The moment I stepped into that hospital room; I felt something leave my body and it never been replaced. Two weeks before my mother passed she and I had a very intense conversation. She wanted me to know how much she loved me. She told me how proud of me she was. She understood my anger and pain. She told me that I was going to have to figure out how to live without the support of my family because they like me. She told me that she thought me to be a good mom. She told me that the world was so much bigger than what I wanted. She encouraged me to enjoy the beauty of life through God's eyes. She apologize to me for my agony and pain. She apologize for purposely attempting to sabotage my life because she wanted me closer. I didn't know how to feel in that moment. I just knew I needed it. I was ready to start over and God decided to take her away from me. My mother died a day before her 59th Birthday. A day after losing her precious cousin Rebekah.

I dedicated this Bible scripture to my mom; Isaiah 61:3, which says, "to provide for those who mourn in Zion; to give them a crown of beauty instead of ashes, festive oil instead of mourning, and splendid clothes instead of despair". The verse continues, "And they will be called righteous trees, planted by the Lord to glorify him".

It is very difficult for me to recount these things and write about them. It exposes my core. Yet, it pushes me to continue because only the truth will sent me free and hopefully free others.

CHAPTER 22

Life after death

They say that life after death of a loved one can cause a range of emotions, including sadness, anger, guilt, and numbness. It can also lead to other effects, such as: shock, unpredictable sleep, isolation forgetfulness and strained relationships. I must say that I experienced all of them and more. My body went into protective mode. Causing me to behave normally and feel numb. I had no problem sleeping. I slept my days away only to wake up long enough to greet my children in the mornings before school and the evenings before their bedtime. Periodically, I would become a drone to binge watching corny sitcoms. Forgetfulness; I would lose time forcing me deeper into depression because I couldn't remember. The brain fog was overtaking my life. I would forget basic tasks like driving directions, where you put things, or when bills are due. Ishaka would step in to encourage me to get better and fast. I couldn't.

Leo would take me on hiking excursion through the wildlife preservations of Jacksonville. His family was very supportive when my own left me to rot. Honestly, I just wanted my mom back. I needed the chance to make it right. My first cousin Michael and his wife made an unannounced visit to my home. I didn't even know that Michael knew where I lived. I welcomed them in my home. The looking upon me recognizing my fractured state. My house was still lavishly decorated but the atmosphere was gloomy; lacking love and laughter that once graced the scene. The kids greeted the two and I excused them into their rooms giving the adults' time to parler.

I offered my unwanted guests a beverage to which they declined. Michael went in to this question and answer session. He wanted to know how I was holding up after losing my mom and having to physically fight with half of my family at the repass. My response to such ridiculous line of questioning was, "Look around cuz. Look at me." He lowered his gaze. His wife sat there like she disgusted at the sight of me. I saw her from the peripheral vision but her no mind. I did however strategically take that opportunity to dispel of a few family lies that were carried on for years about me. I made sure to mention how I was molested at the age of four years old up until I was seven by his sister's now husband.

I poked the topic by saying how they'd all ostracized me; making people believe that I was liar and him never standing up for me. You should have seen the look on his wife's face as the words flowed like melted butter from my mouth. By the end of my tale, she was in tears. Michael's wife turned to him in anger, "You lied to me. You told me that Princess made it all up. I've had this man to my house; around my daughter. Michael how could you?" I sat there laughing, "Yeah Michael, how could you?" He lowered his head; unable to look his wife in the eyes. I watched him cry tears of shame and regret. Michael apologized to me that night and so did his wife. I accepted his apology and asked them to leave my home. Before they got into their car good, I ran to the driveway and politely told Michael, "I didn't treat ya'll like ya'll have treated me. Especially, when ya'll momma died. I honored my aunt Pamela."

Leo never left my side. Every day he would try to reach me; to bring me back to reality. He took care of my children when I couldn't. Alaisja had gone off to school. That shook me up a little. I needed to get well but I couldn't do it in the same city where I'd experienced so much loss and pain. I didn't know what to do. Moving back to New England was an option but not in my current state of mind. I had to figure out what to do. I tried praying. The Bible says that a mustard seed of faith could move a mountain. I was running on fumes; almost out of gas. I leaned on that mustard seed of faith heavy; gave my concerns to God and decided to trust Him. That was my last resort after exhausting myself trying to regain control over my life and failing miserably.

I can't recall the date or time but somewhere during the chaos, I received a call from my cousin Renata. Renata called to check-up on me and the kids. I appreciated her call as it was needed and welcomed. Somehow or another she'd mentioned her new relationship with this pastor without a church. She explained to me that their goal of starting a ministry. They needed funding and wondered if I'd had any experience with grant writing. I was a bit of novice in the area but I was familiar with some of the state-level processes. I told her that could help her.

Renata and I talked over the following weeks about various topics. Being as that Renata is my mother's first cousin, she's a bit older than I. I followed her lead and really wanted to help out. While I was surviving off of crumbs, I still put myself out there to be of service to others. It wasn't something that I necessarily thought about as leading a helping a hand was ingrained in me from childhood. Later learning, that sometimes you can sew seed on foul ground. All the same, Renata made a suggestion that peaked my interest. She offered for me to come to live with her and boyfriend until I got on my feet. I wouldn't have to pay them anything as I would be helping them with solidifying funding for the church.

I don't know why I thought that would be a good idea. Out of desperation and trusting a close family member; I accepted Renata's offer. I packed us up and moved to Alabama.

We weren't there for a week until Renata reneged on our agreement. Perhaps, she didn't like us not wanting to participate in their prayer group. I don't know what the problems was, I didn't even ask. She first came to me and asked for fifty-dollars a week. That was not a problem. She waited a few hours and then came to me asked that I be responsible for the purchase of our food. That wasn't a problem. By the end of the week, after I'd returned to the house I was told that Renata's boyfriend didn't want us there anymore. I didn't question her; I conceded but asked for a week to allow me to find a place. Renata told me that I and my children had to leave that night. I couldn't believe it. My heart broke because I didn't know anything about Alabama. Where was I going to go with my children?

I called Leo and explained to him the situation. He'd told me that moving in with my cousin was bad idea. After he'd saw how my family treated me at my mom's funeral; he couldn't understand how I could ever trust Renata. Leo didn't hit me with *I told you so*. He simply came to get us and we went to his cousin on his father's side Ethel's house. I was familiar with the place as that is where I wouldn't visit him on weekends. I wasn't comfortable with the idea but what choice did I have.

My experience with living with others has never been great. If my own cousin did me like what was I to expect from his family. *God, I am totally trusting you to see us through.* Ethel welcomed us into her home. When we first moved in, things were smooth. I cooked and cleaned the entire home from top to bottom. Every day, there were three hot meals prepared by me. I was able to find a job after living with Ethel for 2 weeks through the old faithful temp service, Randstad. By the third week, I started to see the ill treatment towards my children. I didn't like it. To be honest, I hated it. I had to find a place for us to live and not with someone!

I wasn't comfortable driving to work in Birmingham so I would have Leo take me. The kids were out of school for the summer so they were always at Ethel's house. Leo would take them fishing and stuff like that while I was at work. My children were not happy and neither was I. I spent my days talking to God awaiting his directions. I was miserable but tried to keep a brave face for the kids. My communications with Alaisja really kept me going. Knowing she was away in school was very refreshing.

Going into the fifth week, I had enough money saved to get a place of my own. I couldn't wait to tell the kids that we were now able to move on from there. Ishaka made friends in the neighborhood but he was ready to go! Azariah did not talk much those days; I could tell she was over the whole thing. I called Leo and asked him to help me find an apartment. My online searches were daunting as I knew nothing about the areas. The only thing that popped to mind when think of Birmingham was the First 48 television show. I needed to check each area for registered sex offenders which was quite shocking. It seemed everywhere I'd searched there were way too may registered sex offenders. *Lord help me!*

This was all becoming too much to make sense of. I'd left most of our clothes back in Florida. We were shopping at thrifts stores and clothing drives. It was worse than living in the shelter. I could get my hair done so I decided to grow out my natural hair which I hadn't worn publicly since the rebel stages of my teenagers back in Maryland. I couldn't get my nails done but I learned to appreciate the beauty of my hands with acrylic. My children still have name brand shoes which diminished the stigma of the hand me down clothes; which they never had to wear. My money was low but we were getting by.

Good news finally came when Leo pulled into Ethel's driveway on a hot Alabama Saturday afternoon. "Princess, I think I've found the perfect place. Get the kids and come on." I ran into house and told the kids to come on. I couldn't believe how fast they got up. We made our way to the apartment; low and behold it was perfect. It was in a great area near a Baptist College Campus. There was school within walking distance for kids. There was a bus line nearby which worked out well when my car failed. *I'll take it!*

I told Leo that I wanted the apartment. He gave a slight grin and told that he'd already signed the lease and had paid for the first two months. The place was ours! I jumped whimsically into her big arms landing the biggest kiss upon his sweet lips. *Hallelujah!* God answers prayers like no human being can. I told the kids and they were equally ecstatic. We had no furniture but the place was ours. We got in the car driving to the nearest Wal-Mart to pick up toiletries, bedding, air mattresses and food. This was a happy day; a truly joyous day. I've never seen Ethel and those other folks again!

We didn't have a television but I had my laptop and cellular data. Our first meal was spaghetti bolognese, salad and French bread. We all sat together in a circle on the dining room enjoying the movie Willow as we ate our first meal. I was on the road to recovery. The journey toward mindfulness wellness was hard. Some days I couldn't make heads or tails of my life but I got up every morning plowing through. Leo would do what he could to help me but he couldn't rescue me. This was moment in time that belonged to me and God. I had to lose my mind to regain my senses. I had to lose my possessions to allow the walls of trauma fall. I had to crumble within to find myself. I had to release pain to allow my paradigms to shift. Had I not; no matter what I did, I would always end up back in the same place I was standing in.

At work, I was ridiculed by my co-workers for my clothes as they weren't the finest. I was wearing clothes I'd bought out of the dollar store. I was too thin; so much so I looked sick. There was a rumor going around my family that I had AIDS. It's crazy how some people will treat you when they think you're a nobody with nothing. Even though the rumors and taunting verbal jabs hurt me deeply, I still walked tall. I knew who I was; I just had to remember.

My job was customer service based; assisting others with troubleshooting game cameras. I had no clue as to what a game camera was before starting at EBSCO Industries. I'd heard of EBSCO with regards to research databases, magazines and e-journals. I didn't know that the company was so diversified; which makes them quite successful. At any rate, the game cameras interested me as they introduced me to the world of hunting, fishing and bird watching. As a girl, I would sometimes go out with my grandfather to hunt but I was just a country hanging with her granddaddy. I never paid attention the all of the processes.

Let me describe these game cameras better known as wildlife cameras. They are remote cameras that can be set up outside to take pictures and videos. These cameras operated by batteries that captures images with lightning fast speed. Setup for these cameras is quick and easy. For hunting you would use the cameras to prepare for the trail, count animals, and learn about the wildlife on your property. For wildlife observation you'll capture images of animals in their natural habitat, and gain insights into their habits and behaviors. You can use them for property security to monitor access points and detect people wandering in when they shouldn't be. Other uses would be for land or farm management, gardening, conservation, and more.

I learned everything that I could about cameras especially the brand that we were selling which were high end. My duties were to assist customers who would call in with technical issues there in which I would troubleshoot. I moved from game cameras to feeding which was just as intriguing to me. To be honest, I loved it. The pay wasn't much but I enjoyed the job. It gave my brain a workout. I was also able to rebuild my communication skills. When I tell you that I had a mental breakdown, it was just that. I'd lost the ability to socially communicate while maintaining the topic of conversation. Leo would try to help me but being a high functioning communicator himself; he would often get frustrated with me. Performing my job afforded me the opportunity to hone my skills and expand my knowledge.

My supervisor at EBSCO saw my work and rewarded me greatly. In the middle of my work day and on a call troubleshooting a customer's feeder, my supervisor tapped me on my right shoulder. When Melissa taps you on the shoulder; it's never a good thing. I finished the call and walked over to Melissa's desk. "Hey there Princess," she said in her charming Alabama voice and Delta Burke smile. "Hi Melissa, did you need me for something?" I just knew that

I was about to be let go. "Yes, could you get your things and follow me." Oh lord, I was for sure being fired. Everyone was looking at me, snickering and pointing their fingers my way. I was so embarrassed.

I followed Melissa into the same conference room where I'd be trained. I immediately started to thank her for the opportunity, apologizing for any mistakes that I'd made. Melissa smiled at me. She said, "Princess, you're not being fired. You'll moving to a new team. You'll be paid more money and you won't have to be on the phones." I couldn't believe what I was hearing. I immediately burst out in tears. Melissa appreciated my work ethic, my dependable presence, my tenacity. She told me that she knew I was made to do more. Melissa's words were soul saving in a sense. I needed to hear those words. I didn't know she was that much attention to me. I guess all of the office jokes about me made her take notice. So, with that I say thank you to my busy body co-workers.

I started my new position that day. The role had the same title as the one I'd just been promoted from. I met a feisty five foot four black woman name Anastasia. Anastasia was a fast talking ball of person hyped up on energy drinks. We immediately started our training session which I was more keened to learn processes and software first. However, that is not where Anastasia started. When she missed pronounced *bill of lading* I knew that she was not someone that was equipped to teach me. It would be up to me to learn as much as I could to immediately separate from this women. I mean she'd done her job every day for a few years and couldn't properly pronounce *bill of lading*.

I listened to her and guided the training to optimize my learning. I needed to move through her presentation to allow me access to the nearest computer. Once I was able to login to the software I knew that I could take it from there. I'm a researcher and an avid reader; with those two things working for me, I knew I would excel. As time passed, I slowly gained momentum becoming less likely to be stopped. There

I was back at in thick of things, developing standard operating procedures, educating my counterparts, redeveloping my overall job description to yet again set me apart from the masses.

Life at home, the social dynamic was more than lackluster. While exceling on my job I was drastic failing at home with my children. I was so focused on me getting better, I totally missed the emotional struggle my children were experiencing. I'd become so tight with money, I'd neglected to buy furniture. I hadn't bought my kids any new clothes or shoes for months. They were going to school looking like little rag dolls. I mean my son had holes in the bottom of his shoes. I had to change that. My relationship with Leo had become tumultuous. We barely said two words to one another most days. I cared but I couldn't give that any energy as I needed to focus on my children.

I planned a day out with the kid... ice cream, a walk in the park and little shopping. Ishaka was a reluctant to accept my invitation. He didn't want me to spend any money. I assured him that his selections were well within my budget. Azariah was sure to roam around each store enticed by their offerings. It was a smooth day. Upon returning home, I was greeted with the scowling face Leo presented to me. I paid him no mind and proceeded to make ready for a peaceful evening at home. Dinner and a movie was just what the house needed.

I couldn't believe it things were going great for us in Alabama. Ishaka and Azariah were exceling in school as was I at work. Needless to say, I still had a long wrong ahead me concerning the nightmares. I was in better control of my mental faculties. The performance of operating on auto-pilot had been paused. Relished in the silence within. A quiet is the key to achieving ease, finding balance and calm in a chaotic world. The essential parts of my relationship with Leo were his ability to give me the support needed to recover. Leo was not a goof boyfriend; however, he was a hell of a life coach. He said the things that needed to said even when it hurt. His poised demeanor in the midst of chaos drove me nuts but somehow I became dependent upon it. I knew our relationship wouldn't last so I decided to give him the parts of me that he needed while receiving the parts of him I needed.

Leo was trained in various forms of communication. He practiced meditation techniques that commanded atmospheres. I learned from him. All of the tangible things that I used to hide my fears, pain, etc. were stripped from me. I had to find a more holistic way of dealing with all of the crap. I tried Leo's meditation techniques which bored me to sleep. His way was like one of a Ninja, it was intense. The kids enjoyed though.

I couldn't get with Leo's program so I reverted back to the teachings of the legendary Bob Proctor, the art of mastering self. I combined the teaching of Mr. Proctor and incorporated my Christian faith. Researching meditative sounds I landed upon binaural sounds that promoted healing. I would listen to the binaural sounds while working or reading my books. I was then able to put myself into a meditative state as often needed or wanted.

One evening I decided to stay up while everyone else went to bed. I wanted the quiet time to myself as I had some soul searching to do. I grabbed my cellphone and placed my earbuds in each ear. I turned on the healing sounds and grabbed my Bible. I turned to Isaiah 61:3; beauty for ashes. I allowed my mind to think upon the words I was reading and allowed the God to move through my thoughts. I left myself open; this time not praying for anything but expecting everything. I had to face it all; good and bad. In that moment, I heard the voice again; *Beauty for Ashes*. The question popped into my thought, who do I know that has received *beauty for ashes*?

There it was, the answer... Cinderella. The name Cinderella means girl of ashes. Cinder meaning ashes and Ella meaning girl. I meditated on the story of Cinderella which brought joyful thoughts of childhood memories. It took me back to a place where I first experienced fear. It was like I was back in 1984, sitting on my bedroom floor ready to eat a hotdog, when a splash of blood drop on my sandwich. My four year old little self-sat there staring at the ruined dish. Somehow I'd blocked out the noise of my mother and then boyfriend's fight. My mom was always beating up her boyfriend Jeff. That particular afternoon they had been fighting for hours. Jeff never hit my mom back; he would simply position himself to lessen the effects of her vicious blows. My mom's rage was no joke. My mom took up a knife to stab Jeff but my cousin Laiana attempted to stop her but ended up getting herself stabbed. It was Laiana's blood on that splashed upon my hotdog.

The fighting was close to bedroom if not in my room. I remembered grabbing my Rainbow Brite dolls, running into the furthest corner of my closet, gripping my doll for dear life. I was afraid; not for me but of the atmosphere. Sitting the meditating it was like I my adult self, standing in the room watching all of the action. I saw my little self in that closet holding that doll with my precious eyes closed…praying to God! In that moment, I knew I had to do something. I reached out my right hand for my younger self. I called to me, "Princess." My little self looked up and gave me her hand. I told her that it is was safe to come out of the closet and that there was no need to be afraid anymore. I assured her that I would take care of her. I promised her that I would protect her. We walked out the closet together, hand in hand.

My meditation ended and I opened my eyes with a face full of tears. Identifying the moment when I first experienced fear allowed me to become more compassionate with myself. People always say *give yourself grace*. I've learned that God's grace is sufficient but being compassionate with one's self exposes our courage eliminating the feeling of fear. What I'd also realized during my meditation is that God has always been with me and I with Him. That moment in time was pivotal to my healing. I got up, gave God thanks and went to bed.

A month or so had gone by. I received a totally unexpected phone from a distant family member informing me that Alaisja was pregnant. Two steps forward and ten steps back; the saga of my life. How is she pregnant? I understood how, but HOW! There I was holding my phone in dismay as the voice on the other end continued. I was experiencing an emotional tailspin. My seventeen-year-old daughter was pregnant and so far away from me. I had to get to her. That the distant family member and I told her that I was on my way to Alaisja's school. She stopped me mid-sentence saying, "Alaisja isn't at school. She's at my house." Now why in the heck was my child at her house? Alaisja was supposed to be at school in South Florida. Why was she back in Jacksonville? I hadn't signed her out or given her permission to leave. I gathered myself and asked the woman to send me her address.

I told Leo the news; the entire house was confused. Nevertheless, we packed up a few things and got on the road. I don't see well at night so Leo had to do all of the driving. We made it to Jacksonville, FL from Birmingham, AL in record time. Arriving at my distant cousin home, I was so ready to see my child. It had been months almost a year, since I'd physically seen her face. The door of the home opened up and I was welcomed in. I properly greeted everyone as I searched eagerly for my daughter. I had no clue how long she'd been away from school. I had so many questions but I reserved them. My daughter walked up to me. I barely recognized her. She was so small. She looked malnourished. What had happened to my child?

I wrapped my arms around her and immediately ushered out of the door and into my car. Her siblings welcomed her. We were all excited to see her. Yet, you could look upon all of our faces to see concern. We were concerned for Alaisja. Leo and I checked into a hotel with all of my children. We made the decision to stay for the weekend. Leo opted to stay at his mother's home giving me time alone with my children. The kids and I decided to grab a bite to eat. We went to Applebee's and broke bread together. I watched Alaisja eat her heart out. My child ate so much as if she hadn't eaten in such a long time. I sent her money. She received a stipend from the school. She needed me and couldn't come to me because the last she saw me I was a wreck. What had I done?

After Ishaka and Azariah had gone to sleep, Alaisja and I sat up talking. She was angry with me. I'd abandoned her when she needed me most. My only argument was that I thought she was okay. She told me that she was okay. What hit me the hardest was when she told me that she was six months along in her pregnancy. I couldn't believe it. I was talking to this child almost daily and not once did she mention this to me. She told me that she was doing well in her classes. I asked her if she needed anything. I'd sent her a new comforter set when she asked. We laughed and joked. Not once did she mention her pregnancy. Geesh!

We hung out the entire weekend not telling anyone else that we were in the city. It felt great having all three of my children with me. I was excited to have Alaisja join us in Alabama. I just knew that it would be beneficial to her. I knew that I could assist her with the baby. I banked on being there for her and pulling her back up to the young woman that I knew. The young lady that I'd created. I had a plan for her per usual. I learned quickly that what I wanted for her is what she was running from.

Alaisja was with us in Birmingham for a month before going into labor. I was in the delivery room with daughter as she bore my beautiful granddaughter Alayah Kyrie Fuller. My goodness that was most beautiful baby. I know you may have heard this before but in this case it is a fact; Alayah was born the spitting image of her mother which is the image of Alaisja's father. I was in awe of them. I was scared for my baby girl. I was happy and scared for her. I was the same age as she was when I'd gotten pregnant with her. I never wanted her to experience anything that I'd gone through. That is why I pushed so her so hard. Maybe I'd pushed her away.

I enjoyed having my granddaughter in the house. She was a welcomed presence which we all celebrated. I could tell that Alaisja didn't want to be there. But, I prayed that she would give it chance. She wasn't ready. I'd come home from work late one evening and found Alaisja packing her things into a friend's car. Alayah was only six weeks old and I begged Alaisja to stay. She firmly refused and left my house returning to her daughter's father. I was so afraid for them. All I had was my faith that God would protect and keep them.

Alaisja had been away for about four months. I would send her money via Western Union on a continual basis. I didn't want her to experience any lack. While in the middle of a busy workday, I received a call from Alayah's father. That was the first that I'd heard from him. I was shocked and a little taken aback. I'd found out that he was seven years older than my daughter; I really disliked him for that. I didn't know what to expect from him so I was a bit abrupt. The young man broke down my defences when he said to me that he wanted to be the dad to his daughter that his father was to him. I listened to his presentation and decided to back off, giving them the chance to find their way. I ensured that they knew that I was there for them if they needed me. I can truly say that Alayah's father has shown himself to be a wonderful dad and I have grown to love him as my own.

After speaking with Alayah's dad, Elijah, I decided to visit them stopping first through Jacksonville to see my grandmother. That visit was much needed. I needed to see my granny's face. I gave her the biggest hug. Ishaka and Azariah was too excited to see her as well. I told my granny that I was stopping through on my way to see Alaisja. That woman grabbed her purse so fast and said, "Let's go." I left Ishaka and Azariah with my Aunt so that they could spend time with their cousins. I also didn't know what Alaisja's living situation was and didn't want to expose either of them to a scene they weren't accustomed to.

My granny and I took a nice four hour drive listening to the Blues and music from her era in time. It was a pleasant ride. My granny and I have always gotten along well. I love that lady! She reminded that I was made from a strong woman with other strong women standing behind me. I needed her wisdom. I needed her presence. I needed her love.

As the two us rode together, my granny told me about her health and living conditions. I saw her apartment and looked like a dope house. No one had been there to clean up for her. The place was roach infested and that is now how my granny was accustomed to living. After we visited with Alaisja and her family, I'd decided it was time for me to get back to Jacksonville. My granny needed me.

The kids and I bid our farewells to the few family members we were in touch with. The trip back to Birmingham seemed long. I had so much on my mind. My daughter, grandchild, and my grandmother were all in Florida. They all needed me so I had to make a choice. Leo and I had decided that we were not a good fit for one another. While I would like to say that our relationship ended well; it didn't. Leo returned to Kentucky after I'd found out that he was seeing a close friend of mine. I wasn't made just over it. He wasn't my husband so I didn't expect anything from him when it came to fidelity. I just thought we were better than that. Que sera sera...

I couldn't think about Leo; I had bigger fish to fry. I gave my two week notice to my employer at EBSCO. I really hated to go but I had to. I'd talked to God about it and received my answer, "Go!" I didn't have to fight with the kids; their bags were packed as soon as we returned home from Jacksonville. I cashed in retirement savings that I'd accrued over the years and planned my move. I'd contacted my Auntie Shay back in Jacksonville and commissioned her to find a place an apartment for us. She did just that. She emailed the application and I overnighted the documents to the apartment complex located on the Westside of Jacksonville. I received the approval and commenced to executing my relocation plan.

    I didn't look for a job right away as I had enough money to live for at least a year. By 2018, we were back in Jacksonville, Florida living and thriving. My grandparents moved in with us and life became easy. My homegirl Duvessa invited me out to Dallas, Texas, for a visit. I took her up on the offer. While in Dallas, Duvessa and I came up with a plan to start our tax preparation business. I explained to Duvessa that I currently had a tax prep business, Clear Visions Consulting Services. However, I was down to partner with her and assist where needed.

    Duvessa and I didn't stay in business together after the first tax season; that's less than four months. That season, we'd made one hundred and seventy-five thousand dollars. The plan was for us to take sixty percent of our earnings to pay ourselves and to put the remaining forty percent back into the business. The plan didn't go as mentioned as Duvessa had completely cut me out. This left me to struggle once more. My granny warned me not to trust Duvessa. But, I leaned into my emotions and proceeded business with her without a contract.

    Clear Visions Consulting Services was mine. I had to work it if I was going to keep family afloat. I called on Jesus asking God to make me whole. I put all of my plans before the throne of God and casted my cares upon his shoulders. I went full throttle in business and became quite successful. I had over twelve hundred clients that I worked from corporations to budding entrepreneurs. I put my education, knowledge and skills to work and came out on top.

    You see, sometimes we may fall so deep in the mud that we start to feel like we're stuck. Life has a way of handing out a harsh hand that will slap you around like an egg-sucking dog. You'll start to believe that hype of the pain, the rumors, the lies, the stigma, forgetting that you were born rich. Born rich, fully equipped to overcome the fouls of the world. Somewhere, the dark clouds start to form, backing you into a corner.

I'd been through so much. I'd seen so much. I'd done so many horrible things. I was filthy as a blood clothe. My soul was yearning to be free. I wanted to die. Until one daunting evening, I heard a little voice whisper to my soul, "Princess, you shall live and not die." The day I released myself from the false obligations that held me captive. I was able to understand that I, Princess, was made worthy by the Blood of Jesus. I had a purpose. I am the purpose. God's plan for my life was so much greater than anything that I'd ever experienced. I had been delivered. Redeemed by God's grace. It is my honor to serve the Lord God and to share my testimony with all who have an ear to hear.

Stay Tuned...